CORPORATE
CREDIT

A CFO's Guide to Bank Debt and Loan Agreements

D1488578

Susan C. Alker

Cover design by: Susan Veach
www.doneforyoupublishing.com

Warning – Disclaimer

This book is strictly for informational and educational purposes. The author and/or publisher shall have neither liability nor responsibility to anyone with respect to any loss or damage caused, or alleged to be caused, directly or indirectly by the information contained in this book. The author and/or publisher shall not be liable for any misuse of this material.

Your use of this book does not create an attorney-client relationship with the author, nor does such use constitute the receipt of legal advice from the author. A detailed confidential discussion of your specific circumstances is an integral and necessary component of becoming a client. No user of this book, whether or not the user is an existing client, should act or refrain from acting based on the content of this book without seeking appropriate legal counsel from a properly licensed attorney.

ISBN: 978-0-9845878-0-3

For other articles and publications by Susan C. Alker, please visit the Winston & Strawn LLP website:

www.winston.com

or e-mail Susan:

salker@winston.com

This book is dedicated to
my clients,
the source of so many excellent
ideas and questions.

Acknowledgments

First of all, I would like to thank my husband, Greg Alker, for his support and encouragement throughout the process of getting this book to print. Greg is a deputy district attorney in Los Angeles County, and in the middle of a particularly difficult series of preliminary hearings in a very large case, he took time out to review my drafts and offer suggestions. I am continually grateful for his help.

I'd also like to thank Natalie Alker and Brandon Alker for sharing their good ideas with me, helping me come up with names for titles and chapters, and cheering me on.

Special thanks to Svetlana Attestatova, who had some very helpful suggestions and comments on earlier drafts, to Donna Kozik and her team, who helped me get to the finish line, and to Claire Gomez, who always helps out when help is needed, without complaint.

Thank you to Lisa Kabnick, Chris Olsen, Matt Kirby, Peter Clark, John Iino, and so many other fine lawyers that I've practiced with over the years (too many to name), for being mentors and friends.

Finally, I'd like to thank my partners and colleagues at Winston & Strawn LLP. I am proud to practice law with you.

About the Author

Susan C. Alker is a partner in the Los Angeles office of Winston & Strawn LLP, one of the largest law firms in the world. As a member of the firm's financial industry practice group, she has extensive experience representing major banks, financial institutions, private equity funds, hedge funds, and corporations in a wide variety of lending transactions. Susan frequently advises clients in connection with syndicated credit facilities, leveraged acquisition financings, cross-border loans, asset-based loans, debtor-in-possession credit facilities, investment grade loans, and real estate financings.

In addition, she represents private equity funds in credit facilities for acquisitions and recapitalizations of their portfolio companies, as well as their capital call and subscription lines of credit.

Susan also represents clients in subordinated debt transactions, including mezzanine loans and second-lien loans, and has expertise in dealing with highly complex intercreditor arrangements for sharing of collateral. She also regularly advises clients in workouts and restructurings of credit facilities.

Susan has a JD from the UCLA School of Law and an MBA in international business from California State University, Los Angeles.

Prior to joining Winston & Strawn, she was a member of the corporate finance practice group at O'Melveny & Myers LLP and Reed Smith LLP.

She frequently writes and speaks on topics of interest to financial institutions and corporate borrowers.

Susan is admitted to practice law in California and New York.

Contents

Introduction

I know what you're thinking. Bank loans, huh? This book will be a good choice for those late nights when I'm having trouble getting to sleep. I can't imagine why I would want to read so many pages about loan agreements.

Okay, sure. I get this all the time. When we go to cocktail parties, my husband (who is a criminal prosecutor) gets all the attention. He can talk about the OJ trial or the Phil Spector murder case and keep people fascinated for hours. People hear that I'm a transactional lawyer, and that I work on corporate loans, and they quickly find someone else to talk to!

The fact is, though, there are few things more important to our economy than bank financing. Borrowed money keeps businesses in business, producing products we need, employing people who need jobs, and offering valuable services. Without financing, it would be very difficult for most large companies to survive and grow. Seasonal businesses wouldn't have the cash they need to buy inventory to stock up in time for the day when all the customers show up. Companies that have to pay for supplies up front wouldn't be able to start production. Products wouldn't get made, and people would be out of work.

If you run a business, you know how important financing is. If you're a lender, I don't have to convince you—you're one of the few who would probably stick around to chat with me at a party!

This book was written for corporate officers and others who work at companies that have credit agreements. It will be of particular use to the CFO and those in the accounting department, since they will have day-to-day responsibility for the company's financial matters. It may also be of help to the CEO, in-house legal counsel, and others who get involved in negotiation of the company's loans.

This book will also be helpful for finance professionals who work for banks or other financial institutions. You're probably already familiar with much of what a loan agreement contains, but this guide can help you gain a deeper understanding of the details of what a credit agreement says, where to find particular terms, and what some of the more obscure terms mean. Borrowers and lenders alike need to know whether it's okay for the company to do something, or whether the borrower will need a waiver or written consent from the lender.

You'll notice that throughout the book, I tend to use the term "you" when talking about the borrower. I suppose this just came more naturally to me, since in my law practice I tend to get more questions about these kinds of things from borrowers than from lenders. That doesn't mean that my lender clients don't have questions—they certainly do—but lenders do tend to be a little more familiar with the content of loan agreements already (we'd expect this, since their business is lending money), so their questions come up a little less often. Anyway, don't be offended if you are on the lender side; I'm talking to "you," too!

In this book, I'll give an overview of how a typical credit agreement is structured. I'll let you know where to find some of the most important provisions in the agreement, especially the ones that tell you what you can and can't do, so that you can make sure your company stays in compliance with the terms of your loan agreement. If your company hasn't had a bank loan in the past, you'll be able to use this guide to help navigate your way through the process. If you are responsible for compliance with the terms of a loan agreement, you'll find a helpful form and some guidance for tracking when reports and notices are due to be delivered. If you're thinking about making an acquisition, paying a dividend, or doing something else

outside the normal course of business, this guide will help you iden-
tify which things are typically permitted and which things are likely
to need lender approval before you can go ahead.

Most of all, I'll answer a lot of the questions you are likely to have
about bank debt. I'll explain why certain provisions are included in
loan agreements. Borrowers often want to know why the lender is
so concerned about certain things, or why they are being asked to
do things that on the surface seem rather odd. Understanding the
reasons behind certain loan terms helps with negotiation and with
building the relationship between banker and borrower.

Finally, a word of caution. There's no substitute for having a
good lawyer who regularly handles financial transactions help you
with your financing. This book presents a general overview of the
issues that you're likely to face, but you'll also need specific advice
that relates to you and your business, and that's something that just
can't be found in a book.

Now, let's dive in!

THE BASICS

A bank is a place that will lend you money
if you can prove you don't need it.

~ Bob Hope

PART 1

1

Chapter 1

How to Get a Loan

I want to say just a few words here about obtaining credit for your company, before we move into the specifics of what the terms will be.

Many startup or small companies aren't ready for bank debt right away. Banks are usually looking for three years (or more) of operating history and financial statements that they can review. They also want to see a solid revenue stream and healthy prospects for the future of the business. They want to see experience in operating the business successfully. It takes a while to pull everything together and to be able to demonstrate these things to a prospective lender.

As you know, most companies in the early stages will instead obtain financing from their founders or from outside investors who know and believe in the product or person behind the business. Often, this financing is in the form of an equity investment rather than debt. An equity investment doesn't have to be paid back by any particular time (if ever), but the trade-off is that the investors will have the right to share in the profits and any proceeds from sale of the business, and may want to receive regular dividend payments. The investors may also have a significant say in how the business is managed—particularly if they own enough equity to entitle them to a seat on your board of directors.

When you obtain debt financing from outside sources, it won't usually involve sharing ownership of the business (with some exceptions), but it will require repayment of the amount borrowed, and usually will also require regular payments of interest. Interest is usually payable in cash monthly or quarterly during the entire term of the loan, unless the lender agrees that interest can accrue. Debt financing will place some restrictions on your business (via covenants in the loan agreement) but will not give the lender a direct say in how the business is run.

In the early stages, your company will likely get debt financing from sources other than traditional banks. With non-traditional sources (hedge funds, etc.), flexible terms like long repayment periods and PIK interest (where the interest is "paid-in-kind," meaning it accrues and is added to the outstanding principal amount as if it had been borrowed as part of the loan) are fairly common. Sometimes the lender will also receive warrants to purchase stock in the company or the right to make an equity investment in the company, which gives the lender another potential means for receiving a return on its investment. These options can help reduce the burden of paying a large amount of interest in cash.

As the company grows and develops an attractive operating history, more options become available. For companies that have significant accounts receivable (retail businesses, manufacturers, etc.), factoring can be an option. Factoring is like debt financing, but, as a legal matter, it usually involves the actual sale of your accounts receivable to the factoring company. The factor pays you something like 80% of the face amount of the receivables it is willing to buy (usually your best accounts, that pay on time), and it pays you that amount as soon as the receivable is created. The receivable then belongs to the factoring company, and any amounts paid by the customer go to the factoring company. The benefit for you is that you don't have to wait around to collect payment; you've got it right away—albeit at a discounted price. The factor makes money because it presumably collects close to 100% of the receivable amount, whereas it paid you only 80% (or whatever was negotiated). You may find this attractive because you have the cash in hand much sooner than you otherwise would, and you have off-loaded the risk of non-payment to the factoring company.

Another option is asset-based financing. This is traditional bank financing, but is often easier to obtain than a cash-flow loan (which we'll discuss later). In an asset-based loan, you keep title to all your assets (including accounts receivable), and the lender agrees to loan you money based on the value of certain assets. For example, the lender might say that it will advance up to 80% of the value of your accounts receivable (again, only certain accounts that the lender feels comfortable with), 50% of the value of your finished goods inventory (with some exceptions), 40% of the value of your equipment, etc. The lender will regularly conduct appraisals of these assets, so that if the value changes, it can make sure it hasn't lost the collateral coverage it wanted. (We'll talk more about this in the next chapter.)

Asset-based lenders usually aren't as concerned about the company's revenue and prospects, and they can be more flexible in lending to companies with less attractive financial statements. Asset-based lenders even regularly make loans to companies that are in financial trouble. This is because these lenders know they are protected by your asset value. If necessary, they can foreclose on your assets and sell them in order to be repaid in full. (By the way, this is why it is called an "asset-based" loan; it is based on your asset value, not your cash flow, revenue, or prospects.) Note, though, that some types of service companies or technology companies that don't have assets that are easy to value on a liquidation basis may have a hard time getting asset-based financing.

Finally, if your company does have good financial statements and good prospects, you might qualify for a traditional cash-flow loan from a bank or other financial institution. This is a good position to be in. You can approach several lenders and see which one is able to offer you the best terms. Often, it's easiest to start with the bank that you have your operating accounts with, as the people at that bank know your business and your cash history already.

When considering various lenders, you'll want to think not only about interest rates and fees, but you'll also want to consider the lender's reputation. How does the lender treat its lending customers? Does the lender seem interested in building a long-term relationship with your company? Obviously, if only one lender is willing to lend to you, you'll have to take what you can get. But if you have a choice (and depending on what type of business you're in), a relationship-focused lender can be a good pick. You never know what will happen down the line, and if your company falls on hard times temporarily, you may be better off with a lender who will try to stand by you during that time.

You might also consider what other services the lender can offer you. If you need letters of credit, foreign exchange services, or interest rate swaps and other hedging arrangements, finding a lender that can serve as a one-stop shop can sometimes result in a better deal for you and can make life easier all the way around.

If you don't know any lenders already, ask for introductions. Your company's lawyer and accountant are likely to know several bankers. Other business owners in the same industry may be able to make recommendations. Or, try attending a few local industry conferences. Lenders who attend your industry conferences are very likely to understand your type of business and to be willing to lend to companies in that industry (otherwise, why would they be there?). Bankers want opportunities to lend to good businesses and are generally quite happy to talk to you.

It is worth investing some time to find the right source and the right type of financing for your business.

Chapter 2

What Type of Loan to Get

What type of loan is right for your business? Well, the answer to this is, it depends.

Asset-Based Loans

Many borrowers find asset-based loans to be the best way to go. Asset-based lenders can sometimes offer better pricing than lenders who make loans on a cash flow or revenue basis. This is because they are confident in their first lien security interest on your assets, and they are confident that the value of those assets exceeds the amount of their loan. In any case, they are not loaning you an amount equal to 100% of the value of the assets—rather, they are taking a discount off the top *and* are eliminating certain assets within the class they've chosen to loan against.

For example, the lender might only be willing to make a loan based on your accounts receivable, and within that category, will only loan against receivables from customers who always pay within 90 days and meet other "good credit" criteria. Once you exclude the customer receivables that don't meet the criteria, the total is further discounted to build in a cushion on the value, so perhaps the lender will agree to loan you only up to 80% of the total. The lender will also reserve the right to make additional adjustments or "reserves" for questionable credits. Once all these exclusions are in place, the lender can feel pretty well protected in making this loan. A well-protected lender can offer you a better interest rate, properly reflecting its perceived lower risk in making this loan to you.

On the other hand, asset-based lenders often have stricter requirements as to how you run the business. They will have tightly set financial covenants (typically a fixed charge coverage ratio; more on this later), and they will have tight covenants restricting your ability to take on other debt, make investments, or do other things. In addition to general restrictions on your business, you will probably also be required to process all of your accounts receivable through a lockbox account that is maintained at the lending bank, so that the lender can retain more control over your cash.

Cash-Flow Loans

With a traditional bank loan (also known as a "cash-flow loan," where the credit decision is based more on your cash flow than on your asset value), the pricing may be higher, but you are also likely to get more flexibility in your covenants. Many companies express a preference for cash flow credit, as it is the form of loan that many larger, more mature, stable companies would have—though this depends on what type of business you are in (for example, many retail companies would prefer asset-based credit regardless of their size and operating history).

Unless you are one of the lucky few investment-grade rated companies, the lender will still have a security interest in all your assets. But, in a cash-flow loan, the lender probably won't require a lockbox and is likely to permit you some limited ability to do things like make acquisitions and investments and take on unsecured indebtedness.

Other Financing

As mentioned previously, alternatives like equipment financing or accounts receivable factoring are also worth exploring if your business is not ready for a cash-flow loan and you have valuable assets of these types. The details about these kinds of financing are beyond the scope of this book, but I wanted to mention them so you'll know other options are out there for you if you need them.

Revolving vs. Term

You will probably need a revolving line of credit if you want to use your loan for working capital needs. Most businesses need at least a small line of credit that they can draw on to meet short-term cash requirements. Seasonal businesses in particular can benefit from revolving lines of credit, drawing on the line to order and pay for inventory so that their stores can be stocked up in time for the holiday rush, and then paying the advances back when sales revenue starts coming in.

Term loans are borrowed all at once, up front (though it's possible to delay the funding date or have multiple advances made over time), and can't be re-borrowed once you pay them back. They tend to be more useful for funding major, expensive events like buying a building or acquiring another company. Any transaction that requires you to expend a large amount of cash up front might be a likely candidate for term loan financing. Otherwise, a term loan might be prohibitively expensive (depending on the pricing that you are able to obtain), because even if you don't need all the cash right now, you will have incurred fees and expenses in connection with the loan, and you'll be paying interest on the full amount just for the privilege of having it sit in your bank account.

Chapter 3
Due Diligence, Term Sheets, and Commitments

Now, let's talk about some of the initial matters that come up when you are about to obtain a bank loan.

Due Diligence Review

Any lender considering making a loan to your business will need to conduct a "due diligence" review of your business. This is like an investigation, where the lender takes a close look at your financial statements and accounting records. The lender will also make site visits to your business locations to check out your operations, talk to your managers, and make sure things are as expected. The lender may also talk to your customers, to find out what they think. And, the lender will confirm the existence of the assets that are supposed to serve as collateral for the loan. An asset-based lender will send out appraisers to conduct a very detailed review and prepare a valuation report on your inventory and other assets. If you own realty, you might also need to have an environmental investigation, a site assessment, a survey, and a title report on the property as part of this process.

This process can take some time. It is time well spent, though, because the lender can only offer you the best deal for your business if it understands the business well, feels confident in your management team, and knows exactly what assets you have.

Before you share all this information with the lender, make sure to ask the lender to sign a confidentiality or non-disclosure agreement so that the information about your business won't get out to others. The confidentiality requirement should extend to anyone the lender hires to help it with the review, including accountants, attorneys, and appraisers. Lenders understand the need for these types of agreements and are unlikely to object to your request.

Due diligence usually starts early in the loan process, even before the lender gives you a term sheet listing the proposed terms it intends to offer you for the loan. Even when the lender is finished with its initial review of your business, the lender's counsel may have additional things to review from a legal perspective. Sometimes it seems like the diligence review goes on forever and only stops because it's time to close the deal!

Diligence requests can require a lot of time to respond to and can be burdensome for the company, especially if the accounting department is short-staffed to begin with. Really, it's rare for a company to have an extra person just sitting around with nothing to do other than respond to diligence inquiries from prospective lenders (and we'd probably wonder about management's effectiveness if that were the case). Most lenders understand this and are willing to work with the company to try to minimize the disruption and burden this process can create. It helps to appoint someone to be the primary contact for diligence matters, so that people outside the company (the lender, its counsel, its appraisers, etc.) can all go to one place to get what they need. This saves the outsiders from trying to figure out whom to call, and it saves people at the company from needless interruptions to deal with requests outside of their areas of specialty.

Term Sheets

While the lender is conducting due diligence, the lender will also prepare a draft term sheet. The term sheet will include basic terms such as the loan amount, the interest rate (and how it will be calculated), the payment dates and any prepayment requirements, a description of the security interest the lender will have in the borrower's assets, a statement as to whether any guarantees will be required from others (and whether the guarantees will be secured), and a brief description of the representations and warranties, covenants, financial reports, events of default, indemnification, expense reimbursement, and other terms that will appear in the loan agreement.

The term sheet is often the starting point for negotiations. The borrower can see at a glance if the financial terms of the deal are workable, before significant costs are incurred to document the transaction. Changes are much easier to make at this stage.

At some point during this stage of the deal, the lender's representatives who are working with the company will seek credit approval within the financial institution, so that they know whether they can commit to making the loan on the terms proposed in the term sheet.

Commitment Letters

If the borrower requires it, the lender may issue a commitment letter, committing to provide the loan on the terms stated in the term sheet. Requiring a commitment letter is common in acquisition financings, where the borrower needs assurance that it will have financing available to pay the purchase price for the acquisition when the time comes to close the deal. Whenever the successful closing of another transaction depends on the borrower being able to obtain the financing, it probably makes sense to get a commitment letter. A commitment letter will also be issued if the loan is going to be syndicated (more on this later).

Commitment letters usually include a number of conditions on the commitment—things like no materially adverse events happening to the company before the loan is made, and (possibly) no materially adverse events occurring in the lending market. The conditions will also include the signing of acceptable loan documentation. It's important to remember that despite this being a "commitment," it isn't airtight, and it's possible for the lender to refuse to provide the financing if any of the conditions are not met.

13

A commitment letter for a syndicated loan will also include provisions relating to the role of the agent bank in selecting other lenders for the syndicate, and a section requiring the company to assist in making information available to the other lenders.

Fee Letters

The commitment letter might also be accompanied by a fee letter stating the fees that are owed to the lender or administrative agent in connection with the commitment. If there's only one lender in your deal, the fees might just be stated in the term sheet or commitment letter itself. For syndicated deals, the fees are almost always in a separate letter between the borrower and administrative agent so that they can remain confidential and not be shared with the other lenders.

Sometimes the lender will charge a commitment fee, due upon signing the commitment letter. There might also be an up-front or closing fee, due on the day the transaction closes. Other fees, such as collateral review fees and breakup fees, may also be listed in this letter. In a syndicated deal, the administrative agent will also charge an agency fee, collected quarterly (or sometimes annually) during the term of the loan. In some syndicated deals, you'll have "flex language" in the fee letter, which permits the administrative agent to change the terms of the loan (within agreed-upon limitations) if necessary to complete the syndication of the loan. These terms are often highly negotiated.

This is all just the early part of the loan process, though. The main part of the show is negotiating the credit agreement, which we'll turn to next.

THE CREDIT
AGREEMENT

The length of this document defends it well
against the risk of its being read.

~ Winston Churchill

P
A
R
T

2

Chapter 4
Overview of a Credit Agreement

Most loan agreements follow a recognizable pattern.

Operative Provisions

What we call "operative provisions" are in the front of the loan agreement. Those are the terms that explain how large the credit facility is, what type it is (revolving line of credit or term loan, or both), and how to borrow. For example, there will likely be a section of the loan agreement stating how, when, and where to send notice that you'd like to borrow money. There may also be provisions for how to obtain a letter of credit or a short-term "swingline" loan, as well as an explanation that either of these will reduce availability to borrow under the revolving line of credit.

Repayment of the loan is often addressed right up front in these sections as well. The regularly scheduled principal and interest payment dates will be stated ("the last day of each calendar month" or "the last day of each March, June, September, and December of each fiscal year" or something like that). There may also be some events that trigger prepayment requirements—for example, if you issue new equity or sell significant assets, you might be required to apply some of the proceeds to prepay the debt. (I'll explain all of that later.)

There will be a section explaining how the interest rate will be calculated. Sometimes it's very simple—you pay 7% per annum, and you pay it on the last day of each month. Sometimes it's more complicated, with a choice between the bank's prime rate and a quoted London Interbank Offered Rate (known as "LIBOR") and perhaps even a grid with variable pricing depending on the company's leverage. If you have the option of selecting how the interest rate will be calculated, the method for giving the lender notice of your choice and other details as to the rate calculation will be stated here, too.

There will also be a description of the fees that you'll be required to pay. If you have a revolving line of credit, you'll usually pay a commitment fee or unused line fee. The commitment fee or unused line fee is calculated based on the undrawn (un-borrowed) portion of the line of credit, and is intended to compensate the lender for agreeing to stand by ready to loan you money under the line of credit on a moment's notice.

Closing Conditions

A credit agreement is usually a "sign and close" agreement, meaning there is no time delay between when it is signed and when it becomes effective. There's no period during which the parties work to meet a list of "closing conditions" and where failure to meet them has a legal effect. Regardless of this, a list of closing conditions is nearly always included in a loan agreement. The closing conditions serve the practical purpose of being a guide for preparation for the closing while the agreement is still in draft form and being negotiated. After the deal closes, the list of closing conditions is a helpful record of what was delivered at the closing, in case new parties come along later and need to know which documents might be in the file. If you have a revolving line of credit or letter of credit facility, this section will probably also contain some conditions to borrowing (also known as "conditions to each advance or issuance") and not just the actual "closing" conditions.

Covenants, Representations, and Warranties

Once you get past all these sections about the loan itself, there will be several sections about your company and what you can and can't do. The first section in this part of the agreement is usually the representations and warranties. Here, you'll list a lot of information about your company and the types of assets and liabilities you have. Lenders want to know whether you are keeping your assets in proper condition, and that you don't have significant liabilities in problematic areas like environmental cleanup or multi-employer benefit plans. It is important to review this section and each of the statements in it carefully, to make sure they are accurate. Inaccuracy of a representation at the time you borrow money or sign the loan agreement can be a default under the loan agreement.

Covenants come in two kinds: affirmative and negative. (And, actually, there's a third kind of covenant as well: financial covenants.) The covenants are promises you make as to what you will and will not do with the company after the loan agreement becomes effective. The covenant sections of the agreement will include financial reporting requirements and the applicable financial covenants such as a leverage test or fixed charge coverage test (more on these later).

Defaults

Toward the end of the agreement is a list of items that are "defaults." Defaults will include things like failure to make payments on time, failure to comply with the covenants and other terms of the loan agreement, filing for bankruptcy, and defaulting on other loans (known as a "cross default"). This section of the loan agreement also usually includes a list of things the lender can do if a default occurs (these are called "remedies"). Usually the lender will have whatever rights are available to it by law, plus some other rights— especially the right to sell your assets in connection with a default and foreclosure action, if the loan is secured by a lien on your assets.

Boilerplate

At the back of the agreement are all the "boilerplate" provisions. This includes things like how to obtain amendments and waivers, what state law governs the agreement, confidentiality provisions, waivers of jury trial rights, and a number of other terms that are generally applicable to most loans.

Now we're ready to take a walk through the credit agreement, section by section, to see what it says and answer questions that are frequently asked about its terms.

Chapter 5

How to Borrow Money: Revolving Loans, Term Loans, LCs, and Swinglines

Irecently represented a company that was obtaining its first credit facility. No one at the company had been involved in this kind of thing before, so they were really heading into new territory. This was a fun deal to work on because it represented a new phase in the growth of the company and would open up new possibilities for expanding the business. Throughout the negotiation process, we discussed why the lender needed certain things. We also spent a lot of time thinking about what the company needed, and what it was likely to need in the near future. We wanted to figure out what terms would work best for them, so that the loan agreement wouldn't restrict them from carrying out their plans for the business, while at the same time bearing in mind the lender's legitimate need to protect its interests.

One of the first things we did was sit down and talk through all the basics of how the loan agreement worked, so that the company's officers would understand what they needed to do to get loans and what the lender would expect from them.

Revolver or Term?

Let's start at the beginning. Do you have a revolving loan or a term loan, or both? A revolving loan "revolves"—meaning that you can borrow funds, repay them, and then borrow them back again, over and over, until the loan commitment expires. It's like a revolving door.

A term loan is borrowed all at once (usually) and then is repaid in small segments over time, until it has been paid in full. When you make payments on a term loan, you can't re-borrow those amounts.

Many corporate credit agreements include both a revolving loan facility and a term loan. This makes things a lot easier for the company and lenders alike, as all the terms applicable to the company's loans appear in one place, and all the loans are equally secured by the collateral.

What type of loan you have will affect how you interact with your lender and what other terms will apply to you.

How Do I Borrow Money?

You'll want to take a look at the "borrowing mechanics" section of your loan agreement to find out exactly how to borrow money. This is usually right at the front of the loan agreement, in section 2 or 3. You'll normally get the process going by sending a written notice to the lender or agent (or by giving telephone notice followed by written notice). There will be deadlines stated for when to send the notice ("no later than 10:00 a.m., New York time") and instructions for where to send it. Look for these in your agreement so you'll know ahead of time what you need to do. If your loan bears interest at a rate based on LIBOR (more on this later) you'll usually need to send the notice three days in advance of the date you want to receive the funds. Some loan agreements include a form of borrowing notice that you will fill out; others just say what you need to include in your notice but let you draft up your own form for it.

What Is a Swingline Loan?

A swingline loan is a very short-term revolving loan—usually ten days or less. Swingline loans most often appear in syndicated credit facilities (with multiple lenders) and are made by the agent or other lead lender in the deal. For many companies, the swingline is like an overdraft facility and is just automatically deemed to have been drawn on if the company's operating accounts are underfunded on any given day. This type of loan is included within a larger credit facility for a few reasons: first, the swingline lender will share in a first lien on all of the company's assets right along with the other loans in the credit facility; second, the swingline lender can require the other lenders in the deal to share the risk of nonpayment, thus mitigating its own risk; and third, the fees earned on swingline loans can be significant, so it can be an attractive line of business for the swingline lender.

Swingline loans are made on practically a moment's notice, with minimal documentation. They can be set up so that they are automatically repaid by sweeping cash from the company's deposit accounts the following day. Swingline loans are treated as outstanding revolving loans for purposes of the credit facility. There will usually be a cap on the dollar amount of swingline loans that can be made, and this will be stated as a sub-limit within the overall revolving line of credit. So, for example, the agreement will say that you can have up to $50 million of revolving loans, $10 million of which can be swingline loans. If you've borrowed $5 million of swingline loans, that will mean you can only borrow up to $45 million under the remaining portion of the revolving line of credit.

Letters of Credit: How Can I Get One?

Many companies need letters of credit. Standby letters of credit are just what they sound like: They "stand by" as an assurance of payment, and are frequently used for workers' compensation fund obligations, for support for certain contractual relationships, or to guarantee payment to the landlord for an office space lease.

Companies that import parts or materials from suppliers in other countries often also need trade letters of credit. A trade letter of credit is really an operative payment mechanism rather than a standby assurance of payment. A trade letter of credit is held by the supplier and is actually drawn on each time the supplier ships goods to the company, so that the supplier gets paid in a timely manner, right when the goods are shipped.

It is easier for a company that needs letters of credit to include a letter of credit facility within its primary loan agreement. This is both for convenience and for the lender's protection—since the lender who provides the letters of credit will (similar to a swingline) have the benefit of a first lien security interest in the company's assets and will have the backing of the other lenders in case the borrower does not repay the amounts drawn on the letters of credit.

For the borrower, once you have a secured credit facility in place with a lender who has a first lien on all your assets, it is very difficult, if not impossible, to get a letter of credit from a different lender. That other lender will also need some collateral to support its letter of credit obligation, and will likely require you to deposit cash in an account at its institution to serve as the collateral. Giving the lender this cash collateral may be prohibited under the negative covenants in your senior credit facility (more on this later), so you may need permission from the senior lender to do that.

There will be a rather lengthy set of procedures to follow for obtaining any letter of credit. Usually the issuing lender requires the company to complete its standard application forms before it will issue the letter of credit. Additional fees are also required— typically equivalent to whatever the interest rate margin is on the revolving loan. Note that this fee is calculated using only the "margin" and not the entire interest rate, so, for example, it might be a total of 3%, not LIBOR plus 3%.

Like swingline loans, letters of credit will be treated as outstanding revolving loans for purposes of the credit facility. There will usually be a cap on the dollar amount of all letters of credit that can be issued under the credit facility, and this is set up as a sub-limit within the overall revolving line of credit (for example, the facility will permit up to $25 million of revolving loans, of which up to $5 million may be used for letters of credit).

For purposes of determining whether the maximum amount available under the credit facility for letters of credit has been used up, letters of credit are valued based on their face amount, not on what actually has been drawn. This is because, at least in theory, the beneficiary of the letter of credit could appear at any time and demand the full face amount from the lender.

Chapter 6

Payments

When Are My Payments Due?

It's important to understand how and when payments are to be made under the loan agreement. This is one of those things that you just don't want to get wrong, since being even a few days late can cost you significant additional amounts of money, not to mention possibly subjecting you to other default remedies.

Your loan agreement will have a section that lays out all the details about payments. Some payments are due on a regular schedule. For example, interest payments will always be due on the last day of the month, or the last day of the quarter, or the last day of each "interest period" (usually each quarter).

If you have a term loan, there will be a table that states each date on which an amortization payment of principal is due, and the amount due. This will be hard to miss, as it might take up nearly an entire page of the loan agreement. Amortization can be a straight line across the entire term of the loan, meaning that the amount of each payment is equal. More commonly, amortization payments will vary from year to year, perhaps starting out at a lower level and increasing in later years, with a larger "bullet" or "balloon" payment due on the maturity date. Depending on your company's creditworthiness, you might have a term loan with relatively little amortization (for example, payments of 1% quarterly and then a very large bullet payment at maturity).

Somewhere in this section of the agreement it will probably also say when the loan matures, and that all amounts left outstanding as of the maturity date are due on that day.

There will never be amortization payments due on a revolving loan. The principal amount of a revolving loan is instead just due in full at maturity (unless you go into default and the debt is accelerated).

How to Make Payments

Now let's get into the practical aspects of making payments. Sometimes the lender will send you an invoice before each payment is due. Still, you don't necessarily want to count on that, because if for some reason you don't get the invoice on time, that's not an excuse for not paying on time. It is better if someone in the accounting department sets up a schedule on a calendar, so that no payments are forgotten. This can also help you plan for those times when larger payments, such as amortization of term loan principal, are due. Take a look at the Appendix for an example of a chart that some of my clients have used to help keep track of when payments and reports are due under their loan agreements.

If your lender is also a depositary institution (meaning it is a bank that takes deposits and holds accounts), you might be required to maintain an account at the bank, and the lender might include a provision in the loan agreement that permits it to just debit your account every time a payment is due. As long as you have enough money in your account, this can be a convenient way to handle payments. It pretty much guarantees that you won't be late. For many companies, this is much better than paying by check and risking late arrival of the mail.

If We Have Enough Cash on Hand, Can We Prepay the Loan and Terminate It?

Most loans permit voluntary prepayment of the principal. Sometimes you're allowed to prepay the entire loan (or any part of the loan) "without penalty or premium"—i.e., with no extra fees. But sometimes the loan will have a prepayment penalty. If you have a prepayment penalty, the loan agreement will say that you have to pay something like an extra 3% on any amounts you voluntarily pre-pay within the first year the loan is outstanding, and then 2% in the second year, and so on. Prepayment penalties are meant to help the lender receive something closer to the level of return it expected on the loan. If you pay the loan back early, the lender won't receive all the interest payments it would have received over the subsequent years, so the penalty helps it recoup some of that. Of course, the lender also gets back its principal early and can apply those funds to other uses sooner than expected (and presumably earn some return on those investments), so the amount of the penalty isn't high enough to cover the entire lost interest income stream. Note that a prepayment penalty may also apply to mandatory prepayments of the loan (see below).

Some loans, most often second-lien or other types of loans that are junior to a senior credit facility, might also provide for "no call" periods where the loan may not voluntarily be prepaid at all. This is usually true only in the first year of the loan and not in later periods.

The borrower might have the right to direct that a voluntary pre-payment be applied to the next upcoming payments that would be due, or to any later payments, at its choice, though often the lender requires payments to be applied in inverse order of maturity. All prepayments will have to include accrued interest to the date of pay-ment, so you'll want to take that into account in your calculation of the payment amount.

What Types of Events Trigger a Mandatory Prepayment Requirement?

Some significant events that result in additional cash coming into the company will trigger a mandatory prepayment requirement under the loan. Mandatory prepayment requirements are more often applicable to term loans than revolving lines of credit, partly because amounts prepaid on a revolving line of credit can often just be borrowed right back the next day. That said, occasionally you will see a mandatory prepayment requirement applicable to a revolving loan if it also requires that the revolving line of credit be permanently reduced in size by the amount of the payment (called a "commitment reduction"). This makes the prepayment permanent and eliminates the possibility of re-borrowing those funds. This can create problems for companies that need the availability of the full line of credit in operating their businesses.

Typical mandatory prepayment events would include equity or debt offerings, a significant asset sale or sale of a line of business, receipt of significant insurance or condemnation proceeds, and annual excess cash flow prepayments. Each of these types of events results in a pot of cash appearing at the company. A secured lender will often want the right to require that a portion of this cash (50% or more) be applied to pay down the loan. Sometimes (as with insurance or condemnation proceeds, or asset sales) this is because a portion of the lender's collateral has now left the company—having been sold or destroyed—and those assets have essentially been converted into cash.

Asset sales and insurance/condemnation proceeds are typically required to be applied 100% to prepay the loan, with none of the proceeds left in the company. However, if the company intends to use the cash to purchase other revenue-producing assets, the lender might allow the cash to be applied to that purpose instead of to prepay the loan. Sometimes this can be negotiated into the loan agreement, and sometimes the request has to just be made at the time the event occurs.

Excess cash flow repayments are sometimes required if the company has a lot of debt, as a means of reducing the debt a bit more rapidly over time.

If your loan has an excess cash flow prepayment requirement, you'll want to think carefully about this provision. What constitutes "excess cash flow," as opposed to just cash on hand, is usually the subject of a lot of negotiation, with the company wanting to make sure it is truly "excess" cash that is being applied to the loan and not cash needed in the business. It can get very complicated, with excess cash flow being defined as EBITDA (earnings before interest, taxes, depreciation, and amortization), minus repayments of indebtedness (other than repayments of revolving debt, unless the commitment amount is permanently reduced in connection with such repayments), capital expenditures (possibly net of proceeds of financings for such expenditures), interest expense, and income taxes paid in cash with respect to the applicable period. (Whew!) Sometimes a working capital adjustment is built in to the calculation, to add increases in working capital over the prior year and subtract decreases in working capital as compared to the prior year. Excess cash flow repayments are typically made once a year, based on the annual audited financial statements as of the year end.

Mandatory prepayments are applied to the outstanding debt in the manner described in your loan agreement. Often the lender requires the payment to be applied to the last payments that will be due (in "inverse order") rather than the ones just coming up. Sometimes the payments can be applied pro rata to reduce the amount of each of the remaining amortization payments. This, too, can be negotiated.

Chapter 7

Interest Rates and Lender Fees

Let's talk now about how to calculate your interest rate and fees.

What Is My Interest Rate?

The interest rate provisions are usually found right after (or somewhere near) the payment section, and after the loan mechanics (the "how to borrow" section). Most corporate loan agreements provide for an interest rate based on the London Interbank Offered Rate, known as LIBOR, plus a margin. An alternative rate will probably also be available, at the borrower's election, based on the Base Rate (the lender's prime rate) plus a margin. It also happens sometimes that the interest rate is just a fixed rate ("interest shall accrue at the rate of 7% per annum"), but this would be unusual for a large credit facility.

What Is LIBOR?

The interest rate under most corporate credit agreements is based on LIBOR. This is the rate that banks offer to pay to each other for deposits in United States dollars in the London interbank market. This rate is quoted on an electronic service that the banks subscribe to and is also printed daily in the *Wall Street Journal.* Most often, the definition of LIBOR in your credit agreement will refer to an electronic page called "REUTERS01," which is where most lenders look for LIBOR quotes on the quotation service. LIBOR is a fixed rate for a short period of time. The borrower chooses the "interest period" for which the rate will be fixed—usually one month, two months, or three months (and occasionally six or even nine or twelve months).

Under a standard LIBOR definition, the rate applicable to your loan will be the rate quoted on that electronic page at 11:00 a.m. New York time, two business days before the loan is made (or the interest period begins). The quoted rate, plus the interest rate margin, will be the rate you pay during that period. So, for example, let's say your interest rate margin is 2.75%, and you pick a three-month interest period. If the quoted rate at 11:00 a.m. two business days earlier for three-month LIBOR was 2%, then the rate you will pay during the next three months will be 4.75%. At the end of the three-month period, you can choose again to continue with LIBOR and whether to do a one-month, two-month, or three-month interest period. If you want to get more complicated (and hedge your bets), you can split the loan into several different segments and set different interest periods for each (some long, some short, etc.).

What's the Base Rate, and Why Would We Ever Want It?

This is a really good question. As distinct from LIBOR, a "Base Rate" loan bears interest at a floating rate. The Base Rate itself is usually the lender's quoted prime rate, which is the rate offered to other banks for interbank loans. If the lender is not a bank (and not a member of the Federal Reserve), you can use a *Wall Street Journal* quoted rate or choose a large bank that regularly publishes quotes (Bank of America, Citibank, etc.) and use that bank's quoted rates as the Base Rate for your agreement. Like LIBOR, the actual interest rate you pay will be the defined Base Rate plus an interest rate margin. The interest rate margin on a Base Rate loan is usually lower than the margin for a LIBOR loan, by about 1% (or more). Unlike LIBOR, there are no interest periods, and the rate just floats daily during the term of the loan.

Historically, it has almost always been the case that the Base Rate is higher than LIBOR, so most borrowers would have no reason to choose the Base Rate as their interest rate. So why is it there?

Well, there are a few reasons. First, if you need money quickly, the Base Rate is the way to go. You can usually borrow a Base Rate loan on the same day you ask for it, without advance notice. Just send in your borrowing notice by 10:00 a.m. and get your money by 2:00 p.m. (LIBOR loans, by contrast, usually require two or three business days' advance notice.) The Base Rate option is also helpful if you are borrowing for short periods of time (less than one month) and would otherwise incur breakage costs for ending a LIBOR interest period early.

Another reason for including the option of Base Rate interest is to provide a mechanism for charging interest if LIBOR is somehow unavailable. It would be a real shock if LIBOR were not available as a quoted rate, or if LIBOR loans became illegal, as such things would bring our entire international financial system to a grinding halt. Still, lenders preserve this optional rate just in case disaster ever does strike. Also, you never know, but it is possible that the Base Rate could be lower than LIBOR. It happened in 2008, much to everyone's surprise. Most lenders have added "Base Rate floors" to their definitions of LIBOR, so that even if the quoted LIBOR rate drops below the prime rate (or whatever rate is used as the basis for calculating the Base Rate in the loan agreement), the LIBOR rate that the lender charges you will be equal to the Base Rate at that time. (Some loans include other floors for LIBOR rate loans, too, but for a different reason: to ensure a minimum rate of return on the loan.) So, it's possible that there may come a day when you find Base Rate loans attractive and want to choose this interest rate option.

Default Interest

If the loan goes into default, the borrower will typically owe additional interest at the stated default interest rate. This isn't necessarily automatic, and it might only be triggered by a payment default rather than other types of defaults. Sometimes default interest only applies to the past-due amount, and sometimes it applies to the entire loan.

The default rate is almost always 2% or more above the normal rate applicable to the loan and can be applied immediately upon a default. It is also typical for the lender to require that LIBOR loans convert to Base Rate if the default rate applies. Conversion would occur at the end of the current interest period, to avoid additional costs associated with ending the LIBOR interest period early (and this benefits the company, since you'd otherwise have to pay for the lender's "break funding" costs for terminating the LIBOR interest period before its scheduled ending date).

What Kinds of Fees Can We Expect to Pay?

Commitment fee. A commitment fee is a fee on the unused portion of the revolving line of credit. The lenders charge this fee as the price for keeping funds available to be borrowed by the company on short notice. Since the lenders have to be ready to fund up to the entire amount of your line of credit whenever you send them a borrowing notice, they will charge a fee on that unused but committed amount. Once funds are borrowed, the company pays interest on those amounts and does not pay the commitment fee. One thing to watch out for here is how the "used" portion of the revolving loan commitment is calculated. Letters of credit are usually counted as "used" commitments, and this makes sense because the borrower is already paying an extra fee for the issued letter of credit.

Facility fee. In lieu of (or in addition to) a commitment fee, some lenders charge a facility fee on the entire amount of the revolving commitment, regardless of whether any funds have been borrowed. A facility fee may be set in a lower amount than a commitment fee, since it applies to amounts that have been borrowed and as to which the company also owes interest.

Letter of credit and swingline fees. Use of the other sub-facilities available under a revolving line of credit may trigger additional fees. As mentioned, the letter of credit fee is usually set at the amount of the interest rate margin. The swingline lender may also charge a small fee in addition to the interest payable on the swingline loan.

Up-front fee. Sometimes up-front or closing fees appear in a separate fee letter rather than in the loan agreement itself. The up-front or closing fee is a one-time fee payable at the time the loan closes, and is often paid by deducting the amount from the loan proceeds that are sent to the company on the closing date. In a syndicated deal, there may also be syndication fees or arrangement fees payable at closing.

Agency fee. In a syndicated credit facility, the administrative agent will charge an annual agency fee. This is often stated in a separate fee letter just between the agent and the company, the content of which is not shared with the other lenders. This fee can be payable annually or quarterly, depending on what's negotiated.

There may be other kinds of fees as well, such as collateral management fees (for asset-based loans) and others. These vary from loan to loan. What's most important here is that you understand what the total cost will be, including all of the fees and potential expenses, so that you can determine if the loan makes sense for your business.

Chapter 8

Closing Conditions

Somewhere in the loan agreement (usually right in the middle, which doesn't make much sense) there will be a list of all the documents that the borrower needs to provide to the lender in order to close the deal. There may be other "events" that need to happen before the deal can close, and those will be listed here as well. This section of the agreement is like a checklist of all the tasks that need to be done. This list is the reason why it sometimes seems to take so long to close a loan. There are a lot of things to do!

If you have a revolving line of credit, there will be a much shorter list of additional conditions to each borrowing that apply after the loan closes. Usually this consists of:

> » a certification that the representations and warranties are true as of the date of the borrowing,
> » no default in existence as of the date of the borrowing, and
> » the borrower having delivered a borrowing notice in proper form, requesting the loan.

Delivery of Documents

You'll be required to deliver some essential documents to the lender.

First, you'll need to send copies of all of your "organizational documents"—the articles of incorporation and bylaws, if the company is a corporation, the partnership agreement and certificate of partnership, if it's a partnership, or the limited liability company operating agreement and certificate of formation, if it's a limited liability company. You will also need to deliver a certificate of good standing from the state in which your company is formed, and possibly certificates of good standing from other states in which you operate or are qualified, especially if your company was formed in a different state from where the main office is located. Many corporations are incorporated in Delaware but have their executive offices in another state. The articles of incorporation, certificate of formation, and good standing certificate can be obtained from the secretary of state's office in the applicable state. The lender may want a "certified" copy (certified by the secretary of state) in addition to the copy from your own files. The good standing certificate will need to be dated with a recent date, so even if you have one in your files, you'll usually have to order a new one of those, too. There are service companies that can help with this.

If you have a shareholders' agreement, registration rights agreement, voting rights agreement, outstanding warrants for equity interests in your company, or other similar documents relating to your equity interests, you'll need to provide those as well.

You'll also need board resolutions (or member/manager resolutions, if your company is an LLC, and general partner resolutions if your company is a partnership) approving the loan. A loan is such a significant transaction for a company that it usually requires approval at the highest levels. Precisely who needs to approve the loan depends on your bylaws or what your operating/partnership agreement says. The lender will want to see that the loan was properly approved in order to assure itself that you've taken the required legal steps for a valid loan.

The lender also needs evidence that the people who signed the loan documents, and the people who will sign and deliver requests to borrow money in the future, are authorized by the company to do so. This is important for the company's protection as well, to make sure that unauthorized persons don't draw funds on your loan and direct them to other accounts (also known as stealing!). It's helpful to designate at least two (or more) company officers, in case someone is out sick or on vacation when you need to have something signed. You'll need to certify that they are authorized and provide their officer titles and examples of their signatures.

All of these documents, including the designation of authorized officers, can be delivered to the lender as part of a single corporate secretary's certificate. There are standard forms for this, and they are fairly easy to complete. The corporate secretary and the designated officers just need to sign the certificate and attach all the required documents to it as exhibits.

Loan Documents

Of course, one of the things that needs to happen is that all the loan documents need to be signed by an authorized company officer and delivered to the lender.

Fees and Expenses

On the closing date, you'll need to pay the bank's fees and reimburse it for any expenses incurred prior to that date. If you are borrowing funds on the closing date, the fees can sometimes just be deducted from the amount advanced to you if you arrange for this beforehand with the lender. Some lenders will instead require you to wire funds separately from your account to pay fees and expenses.

Diligence Items

You'll be required to deliver recent financial statements to the lender. If the loan is financing an acquisition, the lender will also want you to prepare (and deliver to them) pro forma financial statements giving effect to the acquisition and loan, to make sure the numbers will still line up well enough after the deal is done. You might also need to provide additional documents about your capital structure and ownership, and perhaps other disclosure items. All of this typically happens fairly early on in the process as part of the lender's due diligence review, so it isn't something you'll need to worry about right before the closing.

Opinions

In most deals, the lender will require a legal opinion. Some transactions with smaller dollar amounts won't have this requirement, but most corporate deals do. The bank's counsel will work with your attorneys on the content of the opinion letter. Usually the opinion letter includes opinions on your corporate existence and authority, absence of conflicts with your organizational documents and other material agreements, enforceability of the loan documents, validity and perfection of the security interest in your assets, and several other matters. Your counsel may need to conduct some additional diligence of its own in order to reach these legal conclusions about your business. If you have subsidiaries in different states, you may need to have your local counsel in each of those states give the corporate opinions as to those companies.

Solvency

Solvency basically means that your company has the ability to pay its debts as they come due, and that the company isn't undercapitalized. In a large acquisition financing, you'll be asked to get a solvency opinion from the investment bank that's advising you on the deal. In other types of deals, you might only be required to deliver a certificate signed by the company's CFO as to the solvency of the company. A lender will not want to make a loan to a company that is insolvent, because if the company were to file for bankruptcy within a relatively short time after the loan is made, the loan could be invalidated by the bankruptcy court. To avoid this risk, which admittedly is rather severe, the lender will want assurances of your solvency, and not just from their own review of your financial records, but in a certificate that they can use later as evidence in a court proceeding if necessary.

Insurance

You'll need to give the lender a set of insurance certificates evidencing all the types of insurance coverage the lender requires. Unlike insurance certificates you would provide for other purposes, these should show the full limits of your coverage. The lender usually asks to be named as an "additional insured" and/or "loss payee" (depending on the type of policy). The lender will likely also want a statement that it will be entitled to notice of cancellation 30 days before the policy terminates. Your insurance agent will be familiar with these requirements and can provide the types of certificates the lender needs. The lender might also request copies of the insurance policies themselves.

Government Authorizations and Consents

If your company is in a regulated industry, you might need consent from the regulators for the transaction. If so, this will be a condition to the closing.

Environmental Reports

If you own real property, the lender may require a Phase I site assessment and certain other environmental certifications about the property. Obtaining these items can take a long time (several weeks at minimum) so this is something you'll want to discuss with your lender early in the process and get started on quickly.

Security Interests

If your loan is secured by a lien on your assets, there will be several other things you need to do to get ready for closing. The lender will require a valid and perfected security interest in your assets on the closing date, and this sometimes requires a lot of steps.

You'll need to deliver original stock certificates for any stock that is being pledged to the lender, together with undated "stock powers executed in blank," which are transfer documents that the

41

lender could use if it ever needed to foreclose on the stock. These should be collected and prepared ahead of time, but not delivered to the lender until the actual closing date.

The lender will conduct searches of public records to see if any-one else has recorded liens on your assets. For personal property (as opposed to realty), there is a registration process with the secretary of state in each state under the Uniform Commercial Code. The lender will usually do the search itself (commonly called a "UCC search"), but it might ask you to do it, in which case your coun-sel or one of the corporate filing services can help you with this. The lender will also prepare UCC-1 financing statements that it will record against your assets. It turns out that it's pretty easy to perfect a security interest in most types of personal property. In addition to executing a security agreement, just file a UCC-1 financing state-ment with the secretary of state in the state in which the company is incorporated, describing the assets covered by the security interest (or "all assets of the debtor" if it's a security interest in everything). There are some kinds of assets that require different steps (more on this later).

If you have registered intellectual property—patents, trade-marks, or copyrights—the lender will probably record its security interest on your registrations at the Patent and Trademark Office or at the Copyright Office. You'll need to sign forms that the lender prepares for this.

If you own vehicles, boats, or heavy equipment that is registered and has a certificate of title, the lender may want to register its secu-rity interest in those assets and may require you to sign forms or other documents and deliver original title certificates.

If you store your inventory in warehouses, or if you lease real property, the lender might require you to obtain bailee letters or landlord waivers. These documents, signed by the warehouse opera-tor or landlord (as applicable), give the lender assurance that its security interest in the assets will be recognized ahead of any inter-ests that the warehouse operator or landlord may obtain by opera-tion of law.

The lender will also require you to obtain deposit account control agreements for your bank accounts, unless the lender is a bank and all your accounts are at that very bank (though sometimes a control agreement will be required even then). Similarly, if you have a securities account at a brokerage (relatively rare for a corporate borrower, but it does come up from time to time), the lender will probably want a control agreement for that account. Since the control agreement requires signatures from the depositary institution where the account is located, obtaining these agreements can take a long time. Again, this is something you'll want to start on early in the process. Sometimes you can get an extension from the lender to deliver these after the closing, but you can't necessarily count on that.

Sometimes the loan agreement will include all the provisions relating to security interests and collateral right in the loan agreement itself, and other times there will be a separate security agreement that includes all of that. The closing conditions related to the security interest might appear in the security agreement instead of in the loan agreement, in which case there might be one simple condition listed in the loan agreement that says you have to meet the conditions set forth in the security agreement.

Real Property

If you own realty, you'll usually need to provide mortgages on the property. If you already have a separate real estate loan just for the property, the lender under your senior credit facility might exclude that property from this requirement, or may want to take a second mortgage on the land. Any time property like this is involved, the deal will take several weeks to close, because there are a lot of steps involved in securing a mortgage on a piece of realty.

The lender will work with a title company to obtain title insurance for the mortgage. They will want to see a title report and perhaps review copies of the documents on record that relate to title exceptions that appear on the report. The lender may conduct an appraisal of the property and may need a flood hazard certificate.

There may also be a separate environmental indemnity agreement for the property. And on and on it goes.

If you lease property, the lender may want the landlord to sign a "Consent and Estoppel" form. This is a fairly straightforward document that gives the lender the right to enter the property and remove the assets that serve as collateral for the loan. There is sometimes some negotiation between the landlord and the lender as to the limitations on this right (the lender will need to agree to pay for repairs if it damages the landlord's property when it removes the items, for example).

If you have any important or significant leases, the lender may also want leasehold mortgages for those. This would apply in a situation where you lease something unusual, like a communications tower (for a television or radio station) or a theater (for a long-term live entertainment production), that is critical to your business and that can't be easily replaced with another property. Most office space is relatively fungible and would not be the subject of a leasehold mortgage; it's assumed that you could always find another building to lease space in if you had to.

Leasehold mortgages involve recording a document called a "memorandum of lease" in the county recorder's office. The memorandum of lease has to be signed by the landlord. Since landlords are often busy with transactions of their own, obtaining the landlord's agreement and signature on your documents can take some time. Again, this is something you'll want to start working on early, so the closing isn't delayed.

Repayment of Other Debt

If you are refinancing an existing credit facility or bond offering, you'll need to let the other lender(s) know, and you'll need to obtain documentation of the termination of that debt. For bonds, there will be a prescribed process for delivering notices and making payments, and this will be stated right in the indenture. Just follow that process. For a regular loan, you'll get a payoff letter from the lender indicating how much money would need to be paid to terminate the loan as of the expected closing date. The letter will need to say that any liens the lender has on your assets will be terminated automatically when the lender receives your payment. It's helpful to include a "per diem" amount in the payoff letter. The per diem amount is the amount of your daily interest accrual, and the letter would say that if your new loan closes a day or two late, you would just need to pay this additional daily amount for each extra day. This is helpful because it means you won't need to go back and get a new letter signed if your closing date is delayed (and, yes, this often happens). Try to get a draft of this letter from the existing lender about a week before the closing date. This will allow time for your new lender to review it and make sure the content is acceptable.

If any existing debt is going to remain outstanding as of the closing date, the new lender may want subordination agreements or intercreditor agreements for that debt. Those terms will be worked out directly between the lenders. If this applies to you, take a look at the section describing subordination and intercreditor terms at the back of this book.

If all of this seems overwhelming to you, you're not alone! Preparing to close a secured credit facility can take quite a bit of work. The process is easier when undertaken as a team effort, including your outside accounting firm and legal counsel as well as a team of people within the company. Experienced legal counsel will be very familiar with all these types of closing requirements and can be of real help to you in getting everything ready.

Chapter 9

Representations and Warranties

A lender needs to know something about your company in order to feel comfortable loaning you millions of dollars. The lender will conduct some due diligence before making the loan, of course, but it will also want you to make statements about the nature of your business and its assets. These statements will appear in the "Representations and Warranties" section of your loan agreement. Representations and warranties are a means of risk allocation. Since you know more about your company than the lender does, the risk that a statement is untrue is allocated to you by having you make the representation.

The representations and warranties are usually made as of the closing date (the date you sign the agreement) and as of the date any funds are advanced. For a term loan, these two dates are often the same—or very close together. For a revolving line of credit, you might borrow many times during the course of a year, and each time you draw funds the representations are deemed to be made again. This means you need to make sure that you are in compliance with the representations pretty much all the time, if you want to keep borrowing money. (On a related note, take a close look at the monthly or quarterly compliance certificates you are expected to deliver with your financial statements. Sometimes they include a statement that the representations and warranties are true as of the date of the certificate, regardless of whether any borrowings were made on that day.) The bottom line is that your representations and warranties aren't necessarily over and done with as of the closing.

The representations and warranties should generally be statements that you, as a corporate officer, would fairly readily know to be true. You'll want to carefully review them and make sure they are indeed true in every respect.

Many of the representations are qualified by schedules that are attached at the back of the agreement. For example, you might make a representation that "as of the Closing Date, all of the subsidiaries of the Company are listed on Schedule 5.1 hereto" and then at the back of the agreement, Schedule 5.1 would contain a list of all of your subsidiaries. Or, the representation might refer to the schedule for a list of exceptions to the representation (for example, "except as set forth on Schedule 5.5 hereto, each Material Agreement is in full force and effect"; in that case, Schedule 5.5 might just say "None" on it if there were no reason to think any of the agreements had been terminated).

Many times, preparation of the schedules is one of the most time-consuming tasks the company encounters in connection with getting the loan. There will be schedules for the representations and warranties as described here, and then a separate set of schedules relating to the security interest in the collateral. If the schedule requirements seem too burdensome, it may be possible to reword some of the requirements to limit them to "material" items rather than "all" items in a category. Some schedules might be eliminated altogether, depending on the relative importance of the content. These are points for negotiation.

The representations will cover several things about your company, like corporate existence, ERISA (Employee Retirement Income Security Act) benefit plans, environmental issues, litigation, real property, taxes, and other things.

Corporate Existence, Powers, Qualification

You will be required to state that your company is a corporation (or partnership, etc.), that is duly organized and validly existing under the laws of its state of incorporation, and that it is in good standing under that state's laws. You'll also be asked to state that the company has the required power and authority to carry on its business and to enter into and perform its obligations under the credit agreement and related documents. You might also be asked to represent that the company and its subsidiaries are properly qualified to do business in each state where they operate, and that they are in good standing in each of those states as well.

Subsidiaries

If the company has subsidiaries, you'll be asked to make representations about the ownership of their equity interests (does the company own 100% of the equity, or are there other stockholders?), and you'll need to make the same representations as to existence, good standing, and corporate power and authority of each subsidiary as the ones made about the company.

No Conflict

This representation is about conflicts between the loan agreement and other documents. You'll be asked to state that the execution, delivery, and performance of the loan documents won't conflict with your articles of incorporation or bylaws, any court decrees or government rules or regulations applicable to your business, or any material agreements you are already a party to. You will also represent that entering into the loan agreement will not trigger imposition of a lien on any of your assets (other than liens in favor of this lender) or require consent of third parties, other than consents that have been obtained at the time of closing.

Binding Obligation

This one always sounds a little odd, but you are asked to represent that the loan documents are valid and binding obligations, enforceable against you in accordance with their terms, except where bankruptcy or other similar laws would limit enforceability. Usually, your counsel will be asked to give a legal opinion on this topic as well, and there are standard conventions among legal counsel for how this is addressed.

Financial Condition

The agreement will include a representation that the latest set of financial statements you delivered to the lender was prepared in accordance with generally accepted accounting principles (commonly known as "GAAP") and "fairly present, in all material respects, the financial position of the company for the period then ended." This is standard language and is meant to protect the lender in case your financial statements turn out to have been faulty or need to be restated later. The lender relies heavily on your financial statements in making its credit decision, so this is an important representation.

No Material Adverse Change

This representation will say that since the date of the audited financial statements mentioned in the financial condition representation, no event has occurred that has resulted in a material adverse effect. All well and good, but what's a material adverse effect? The definition varies (and sometimes gets negotiated), but it usually says something like the following:

(a) a material adverse effect on the business, operations, properties, assets or condition (financial or otherwise) of the company and its subsidiaries taken as a whole, or

(b) impairment of the company's ability to perform, or of the lender to enforce, the obligations under the loan agreement.

Title to Properties; Assets

You'll be asked to make representations about your assets. These sometimes take different forms, depending on how the loan agreement is drafted. Sometimes these representations will appear in the security agreement rather than here, or they will be in a separate section of the loan agreement that relates to the security interest. But generally there will be a representation that you own your assets and that they are kept in proper working order for use in your business.

Materiality

The content of the representations and warranties section is subject to significant negotiation between the borrower and lender. The borrower will usually want to try to include materiality carve outs in the representations in as many places as possible—so, for example, it's not just "there is no litigation pending against the company" but rather "there is no litigation pending against the company that could reasonably be expected to have a material adverse effect." The lender will often accept these kinds of changes as to certain types of representations, but not as to all of them. Some representations are so often qualified by materiality that the lender's loan agreement form may already have this built in (as is often the case with a litigation representation, for example).

Materiality standards are necessary in some cases just to eliminate things that the lender doesn't care much about but that would be burdensome for the borrower to determine. For example, a representation that says that "the company has no intellectual property other than as listed on Schedule 5.9 to the loan agreement" would result in someone at the company spending countless hours trying to prepare a complete schedule. This wouldn't be a good use of anyone's time. The lender likely only cares about material intellectual property anyway. For most companies, material intellectual property would consist of patents, copyrights, or trademarks that are formally registered at the Patent and Trademark Office or the Copyright Office in Washington, D.C. A representation like this could be modified to read "the company has no material intellectual property [or no registered patents, trademarks, or copyrights, or applications for registration] other than as listed on Schedule 5.9." It's often important that the time and effort required to make representations be considered and addressed by both parties to the agreement.

Chapter 10

Reporting Requirements

Members of the accounting department will need to pay close attention to the many reporting requirements in the loan agreement. I sometimes give my borrower clients a chart they can use to list all the dates when reports and notices are due, so that they can easily track what is due when. The chart can also include all the one-time events that might happen that would trigger some kind of reporting or payment to be made. This cheat sheet is a handy thing to have around, especially for a new loan where the company isn't already used to the terms. A template you can use for this purpose is in the Appendix.

Financial Statements

Before the credit agreement is signed, make sure the person who will be responsible for delivering the reports has read the draft agreement and has determined that the company actually can perform the required tasks by the deadlines set for each of them. For example, if your company is privately held, producing audited financial statements within 90 days after the end of your fiscal year may be very difficult (unless your fiscal year ends at an odd time when accountants aren't too busy—like July). Public companies are required by the SEC to produce audited financials within 90 days after the end of the year, and since so many companies align their fiscal years with the calendar year, this makes for an extremely busy time for auditors between January and the end of March. Your company, if privately held, is unlikely to get much attention from those overworked auditing teams until after March 31st. Fortunately, many lenders understand this and are willing to give private companies some extra time.

There may also be some flexibility as to other reporting requirements. You'll just have to ask to find out. Most of the time, the lender is not going to be interested in creating hair-trigger defaults by setting unrealistic deadlines and waiting for you to fail to meet them. The lender usually just wants to receive the information—and to receive it while it's still relevant. There is sometimes some possibility for additional days to deliver something if you find it burdensome to meet the requirement the lender initially proposes. For example, accounts receivable reports may be too difficult for you to produce within ten days of the month end, but maybe you routinely have them ready by the 15th. Ask the lender to set the requirement at the 15th and make your life a whole lot easier.

Are There Other Events I Have to Report On?

Yes! Your loan agreement likely sets out a list of things that you'll need to send a notice (or report) to the lenders about. It's helpful to familiarize yourself with the types of things your lender wants to know about, so that if something like this occurs, you'll remember that you may have to do something under your loan agreement. Then you can look up the details when the event happens and figure out what to do. Many companies have gone into default under their loan agreements by inadvertently failing to deliver notices when required.

Typical events that trigger reports or notices include: events of default or potential events of default, any public filings with the SEC, filing of any significant litigation against the company (or a credible threat of such a filing), any employee benefit plan problem (including receipt of notices relating to multi-employer benefit plans), material changes in insurance coverage, receipt of any notice from a government agency or regulatory body (whether in the ordinary course of business or not), formation of a new subsidiary, entering into a new material contract, receiving notices from any holder of subordinated debt, plans to amend your articles of incorporation, and many other types of things. These things are easy to forget about, which is why I suggest you include them in a chart like the one shown in the Appendix.

Chapter 11

Financial Covenants

If you are a CFO or accountant, this is the section of the loan agreement that you'll probably gravitate toward first. Here's where all the numbers are and where the rubber really meets the road. The financial covenants in your loan agreement test your company's performance in several different ways. Depending on the type of loan you have, and what industry you're in, you may have more (or different) financial tests.

Lenders find these covenant tests very useful in determining how well the company is performing and whether the company's earnings are sufficient given the amount of its liabilities. The covenant levels are set based on the company's projections, but there's usually a reasonable cushion built in, in case the company was too optimistic in thinking about its future. Failure to meet the tests can give the lender warning of an impending problem with the company's overall performance, long before the problem leads to a payment default. Of course, failure to meet the covenant tests is, in itself, a default under the loan agreement.

EBITDA

First, let's consider how financial covenants are calculated. Many of the financial covenants will use "Consolidated EBITDA" as the basis for calculation of the ratios. EBITDA (which stands for earnings before interest, taxes, depreciation, and amortization) is a helpful measurement because it approximates the amount of cash being generated by the company. You won't find EBITDA as a line item on the company's financial statements, because it's not a term recognized in GAAP. So, it will need to be calculated separately.

To get to EBITDA, we start with the company's revenue. This generally leads us to what lenders refer to as "Consolidated Net Income." This may be a separately defined term in the loan agreement. Consolidated Net Income means, for example, the net income of the company and its subsidiaries, excluding (i) income or loss of joint ventures, any entity prior to the date it became a subsidiary of the company, and subsidiaries restricted from paying dividends to the company, (ii) after-tax gains or losses from the sale of assets or returned surplus assets of a pension plan, and (iii) net extraordinary gains or non-cash extraordinary losses.

"Consolidated EBITDA" then starts with the defined term Consolidated Net Income and adjusts further to add back non-cash items. Here's a typical definition (in legalese), with many non-cash adjustments included:

> <u>Consolidated Adjusted EBITDA</u> means, for any period, the sum (without duplication) of the amounts for such period of (i) Consolidated Net Income, (ii) Consolidated Interest Expense, (iii) provisions for taxes based on income, (iv) total depreciation expense, (v) total amortization expense, and (vi) other non-cash items (other than any such non-cash item to the extent it represents an accrual of or reserve for cash expenditures in any future period), but only, in the case of clauses (ii) through (vi) above, to the extent deducted in the calculation of Consolidated Net Income, <u>less</u> other non-cash items added in the calculation of Consolidated Net Income (other than any such non-cash item to the extent it will result in the receipt of cash payments in any future period), all of the foregoing as determined on a consolidated basis for the Company and its Subsidiaries in conformity with GAAP.

Leverage Ratio

A lender usually wants to know how the company's EBITDA stacks up against the amount of debt the company has taken on.

There is also usually an assumption that the company will reduce the principal amount of its debt over time. So, there will be a test comparing debt to EBITDA, and the maximum level of debt permitted will be set at lower levels over time.

For example (and please note that this is just an example; all of these numbers would be set specifically for your company, based on your operations):

> The Company shall not permit the ratio of (a) Consolidated Total Debt to (b) Consolidated EBITDA for the four consecutive fiscal quarter period ending on the last day of any fiscal quarter, as of the last day of each fiscal quarter ending during the periods set forth below, to exceed the ratio indicated:

Period	Maximum Leverage Ratio
1/1/10 – 12/31/10	3:00:1.00
1/1/11 – 6/30/11	2.75:1.00
6/30/11 and thereafter	2.00:1.00

Note that leverage can be calculated based on the company's total debt or based only on senior debt, or both. Senior debt usually excludes any debt that is junior or subordinated.

Interest Coverage Ratio

Similar to the leverage test, a lender may also want to test the ratio of EBITDA to interest expense. The calculation of EBITDA (as shown above) adds back interest expense to the net income figure, so it is a fair starting point. Note that the interest coverage test is a minimum test (you have to maintain at least this much coverage), whereas leverage is always set up as a maximum test (you can't have more than the number indicated). Because interest is a cash expense that has to be paid regularly, it is important to know that the company will have enough money available to pay this expense along with all its other operating costs. (Again, as with all of these covenants, the numbers shown are just examples and not meant to indicate what appropriate covenant levels would be for your company.)

The Company shall not permit the ratio of (i) Consolidated EBITDA to (ii) Consolidated Interest Expense for any four fiscal quarter period ending during the periods set forth below to be less than the ratio indicated:

Period	Minimum Interest Coverage Ratio
1/1/10 – 12/31/10	2.00:1.00
1/1/11 – 6/30/11	2.25:1.00
6/30/11 and thereafter	2.75:1.00

Fixed Charge Coverage Ratio

Commonly used in asset-based loans, the fixed charge coverage ratio takes into consideration many other types of expenses and obligations that the borrower will incur in its business. The definition of "Consolidated Fixed Charges" can be negotiated to include or exclude certain things of particular significance to the company. Typically, "Consolidated Fixed Charges" includes interest expense, provisions for taxes based on income, scheduled principal payments in respect of indebtedness, dividends (or other permitted payments in respect of equity), rents paid or payable during the relevant period under capital leases, and (possibly) capital expenditures and payments to affiliates.

The Company shall not permit the ratio of (i) Consolidated EBITDA to (ii) Consolidated Fixed Charges for any four fiscal quarter period ending during any of the periods set forth below to be less than the ratio indicated:

Period	Minimum Fixed Charge Coverage Ratio
1/1/10 – 12/31/10	1.50:1.00
1/1/11 – 6/30/11	1.60:1.00
6/30/11 and thereafter	1.70:1.00

Minimum EBITDA

Sometimes, in addition to the ratios, the lender will want to ensure that the company continues to produce EBITDA at certain levels. The level required may vary during the term of the agreement, especially for companies with seasonal revenue streams.

Minimum Net Worth

There might also be a requirement for a minimum amount of net worth. There can be a bit of negotiation over the definition of this term, but usually it's pretty straightforward: capital stock, plus paid-in capital, plus all or some percentage of retained earnings (minus accumulated deficits).

Capital Expenditures

Capital expenditures may be restricted in the financial covenants section or in the negative covenants section of the loan agreement. Either way, many companies are subject to limitations on how much they can spend for this purpose. This is almost always expressed as an annual basket amount (for example, you can spend up to $1 million on capital assets in fiscal year 2010, up to $1.25 million in 2011, and so on). The numbers will be based on your historic expenditure levels and your plans for the coming years, as negotiated between you and the lender. Capital expenditures will include all expenditures for capital assets, whether you pay in cash or finance the purchase. (Note that if you finance the purchase, the financing also has to be permitted in the negative covenant sections that otherwise restrict your ability to incur debt and liens.) Some loan agreements include a carry-over of amounts not spent in the current year, which can give you a little more flexibility as to when you make purchases. This means that, in the example above, if you only spent $500,000 on capital assets in 2010, you could add the remaining $500,000 to the permitted amount for 2011 (but not for subsequent years) and spend up to $1.75 million in 2011.

Other

There are some other types of financial covenants that your lender may require. These can vary a lot, depending on the type of loan and type of business you have, and will likely be negotiated very specifically with your business in mind.

Chapter 12

Affirmative Covenants

Covenants are divided into two types: affirmative covenants, meaning things you have to do "affirmatively," and negative covenants, which are things you can't do. (Financial covenants are frequently included in the negative covenant section of the loan agreement, though they also can stand alone in their own category.) Almost any requirement can be worded as a positive "you must do this" or as a negative "you must not fail or neglect to do this," and so some of the things that appear in the category of an affirmative or negative covenant could probably just as easily have been put in the other category. There isn't always a strong logic as to why something is in one section or the other, but there is a common practice for what types of things go in each place. We'll address the topics in the sections in which they would normally appear in a loan agreement, based on market convention.

Notices and Deliveries

As mentioned above, the reporting requirements might appear in their own separate section of the loan agreement, or they might appear as the first few items in the list of affirmative covenants. Since we've already discussed all of these in the previous chapter, we won't get into the details again here.

Corporate Existence

There will be a requirement that you maintain your company's existence and its good standing in the states where you're doing business. This covenant might also include a requirement to maintain all material rights and franchises that are important for the business. The lender wants to know that the company will still exist (no surprise there) and that it is continuing to operate as expected.

Payment of Taxes

Your lender will want to know that you are staying current on tax payments, because the government can take a lien on your assets for the amount of the tax if you fail to pay. So, there is usually a requirement that you will pay all your corporate taxes on time, except for amounts that you are disputing in good faith and have taken reserves for in your financial statements.

Maintenance of Properties, Insurance, Etc.

In a secured loan, it is common to have covenants relating to your assets. The lender wants you to continue to own all the assets you need in order to run the business, and will often require the assets to be "in good repair" or "in working order" to make sure that you can use the assets to continue to produce revenue. There may also be a specific covenant about undertaking appropriate repairs and maintenance for these assets.

In addition, the lender will want to know that you are maintaining appropriate insurance coverage for the business. This applies not just to your assets (insurance against casualty events like fire, flood, or other destruction of the assets) but also to liability insurance and business interruption insurance. Sometimes the lender will also require a "key person" policy (formerly known as a "key man" policy) be obtained on the life of one or more of the managers who are critical to the company's business. In that case, the policy will usually be assigned directly to the lender. You will be required to give the lender certificates evidencing your insurance coverage both at closing and at regular intervals (usually annually) during the term of the loan. Asset-based loans will often include stricter requirements for insurance than cash-flow loans.

Inspection and Visitation Rights

The lender will want the right to visit your offices from time to time. In an asset-based loan, the lender will require you to permit regular visits and appraisals of the assets, with a team on site at your various locations. Even cash-flow lenders will usually require you to agree to let them inspect your books and records regularly. The topic most at issue in this covenant will be how many visits are to be paid for by the borrower versus those conducted at the lender's own cost. The borrower usually does not have concerns about allowing the lender to visit for a reasonable number of times, but it does not want to pay for the costs of duplicate visits. Note, however, that if the borrower is in default, it is customary to permit any number of visits and inspections at the borrower's cost. Visits to your business locations usually require reasonable advance notice. You can also require that visits be conducted during your normal business hours, and that authorized company representatives be present for any discussions with outside auditors and customers.

Environmental Issues

There will usually be a rather lengthy covenant about environmental issues. The lender will want the borrower to deliver copies of any notices or communications relating to environmental concerns, and copies of environmental audits. The borrower will also be required to maintain environmental review programs and take other actions necessary to abide by regulatory requirements. Some credit facilities will require environmental audits to be undertaken, and this is most common where there is a known environmental problem at one of the borrower's locations. Loans secured by real estate will have additional environmental provisions, as this is an area where potential liability can be very significant. The liability can, in some cases, be asserted by the injured party directly against the lender as well as against the borrower. Because of the potential for liability, lenders are often concerned about this area and will request more detailed representations than for other topics.

Subsidiaries

If the company forms or acquires new subsidiaries after the closing, the company may be required to have them sign guarantees, in order to add them as guarantors of the loan. If the loan is secured, the borrower may also need to have them execute counterparts to the security agreement, in order to grant liens on all their assets. The borrower (the parent company, in this case) will also need to pledge the stock of each of its subsidiaries as collateral for the loan.

Having a subsidiary guarantee the loan and pledge its assets in support of the loan gives the lender additional collateral and additional means for repayment of its loan. This also gives the borrower additional flexibility because the borrower is usually permitted to transfer assets and to make intercompany investments (including loans) between subsidiaries that are guarantors of the loan—but would be restricted from doing so with non-guarantor subsidiaries. As long as the lender has a lien on all the assets and a guarantee from all the companies, the lender is unlikely to be concerned about which company is holding those assets at any particular time.

These terms requiring subsidiaries to provide guarantees and to grant security interests in their assets often will not apply to foreign subsidiaries. This is because of a tax rule that, under certain conditions, could require the U.S.-based parent company to treat the amount of a guarantee provided by its foreign subsidiary as a dividend payment—just as if the subsidiary had sent a cash dividend to the parent in this amount. Of course, no cash would be changing hands here, so having the parent company owe taxes on this amount is undesirable, to say the least! Most lenders will agree to eliminate these requirements as to foreign subsidiaries so that the company will not incur this extra tax burden. It is generally permissible to pledge up to 65% of the subsidiary's stock in support of the loan without creating a tax issue, so many credit agreements do include a limited stock pledge requirement for up to 65% of the foreign subsidiary's stock. If you have foreign subsidiaries, make sure to check with a tax lawyer to see which of the rules apply to you and what the impact could be for your company. If a significant amount of your company's value is in a foreign subsidiary, you will need additional guidance as to how a loan could be structured to work in that situation.

Hedging

If you have a large syndicated term loan, you might be required to purchase an interest rate hedge as to 50% or more of the loan amount. The purpose of the hedge is to protect the company against large fluctuations in the interest rate, to make sure the company doesn't suddenly get overburdened by very large interest payments as a result of market conditions. You can theoretically get an interest rate hedge or swap contract from any swap provider, but since most providers will require collateral, it is easiest to get the hedge or swap from one of the lenders under the credit facility. The security agreement will usually provide for swap or hedging arrangements provided by a lender under the credit facility (or one of its affiliates) to be secured by the collateral right along with any loans that are made, so the collateral issue is already taken care of for any such lender.

Deposit Accounts

If you have a loan from a single lender (not a syndicated deal) and the lender is a bank that typically provides treasury services and maintains deposit accounts, the lender may require you to maintain your primary banking relationship at its institution. This makes loan and payment processing easier, but it also gives the lender a quicker means for controlling your cash if you go into default. Indeed, it is common in asset-based loans for the lender to require you to process all of your accounts receivable through a lockbox account that the lender controls.

In any type of loan agreement for a secured loan, you will usually be required to provide the lender with control agreements for each of your deposit accounts. A control agreement is a three-way agreement between the borrower (depositor), the lender (secured party), and the depositary institution (the bank where the account is held, which in some cases could be the same as the lender). Unless the account is held at the lending institution, this agreement will be necessary in order for the lender to perfect its security interest in the account. It gives the lender the ability to take control of the account if the borrower goes into default. Practically speaking, most lenders wouldn't immediately seize the borrower's bank accounts if the borrower missed a reporting deadline or failed to meet a financial covenant for one quarter, but the lender has this right and can be expected to use it if there's a significant default—especially if there is concern about your ability to repay the loan otherwise. A typical control agreement does not give the lender the ability to control the account outside of a default situation, except as to an account that is intended to function as a lockbox (with the lender having control of the account from day one, typical for an asset-based loan).

The requirement for control agreements may appear in the security agreement, but it is more commonly found in the affirmative covenants section of the loan agreement itself.

Chapter 13

Negative Covenants

Okay, now we've reached the real heart of your agreement. Most of the questions I get about loan terms are about the content of the negative covenants. That's probably because this section has all the "thou shalt not" limitations in it. All those questions about what you can do, and what you can't do, get answered here.

Other Debt

A lender likes to have limitations on the amount of debt a company can take on. This is partly addressed in the leverage test in the financial covenants section described earlier, but that's just a general test of overall leverage. It usually is too general for these purposes, and it probably includes too much cushion to serve as the only limitation. The loan agreement will likely contain a strongly worded prohibition on taking on other debt, and then will list certain types of debt that are permitted exceptions to the rule.

Though large amounts of existing debt will probably need to be repaid and terminated when this new loan goes into effect, it is common to permit the continued existence of reasonably small amounts of other debt already in place, reasonable amounts of specialized forms of debt (like equipment financings), and junior debt that is being entered into at the same time as this loan agreement. This existing debt will usually be listed on a schedule at the back of the loan agreement. Permission to maintain this debt will include any refinancings as well, with the principal amount capped. The company will usually be permitted to have some equipment financings, as long as the only security interest that the finance provider obtains is a lien on the equipment itself. Often there will also be a cap on the overall amount of this type of debt. The company may also be permitted to have intercompany debt between itself and its subsidiaries, which may be unlimited in amount if the subsidiaries have guaranteed the loan and granted liens on their assets, as explained previously, or up to a capped amount if the subsidiaries have not guaranteed the loan. It is also not unusual to permit the company to be liable for indebtedness that it assumes in connection with the purchase of an asset, so long as the purchase itself was permitted under the loan agreement (subject to certain other conditions).

Permission to have and incur other types of debt is often negotiated on a case-by-case basis, depending on the type of business the company is in and its anticipated needs.

Other Liens

Like the debt covenant, the company will usually be prohibited from granting any liens on its property, with a few narrow exceptions.

There will nearly always be exceptions for immaterial liens that commonly arise by operation of law, such as materialmen's or warehousemen's liens, liens for certain types of easements or minor encroachments, statutory liens arising in favor of landlords and banks, deposits for worker's compensation or unemployment insurance, license or subleases of property, and other similar things. Lenders understand that these types of liens arise in the normal course of business for most companies and are not overly concerned about this.

Similar to the debt covenant, it is fairly common to permit reasonable liens in existence as of the closing date, and liens on assets acquired after the closing, based on certain conditions. It is not typical for a lender to permit any significant other liens to be granted, especially liens with respect to other indebtedness, though larger companies can often negotiate a basket for a relatively small amount of indebtedness that can be secured by liens.

What Is a Negative Pledge?

A prohibition on liens is more restrictive than a negative pledge, so that is usually the preferred method a lender would use to protect its secured position. But, you might have an agreement that has a negative pledge instead of—or in addition to—a lien covenant.

The negative pledge provision will work in favor of the lender and will provide that, although the lender is going to be unsecured as to this loan, if any other debt of the company is secured (whether now or at a later date), then this loan must also be secured on the same basis as that other debt. This is common in high-end investment grade credits. In this case, the lender is okay with having its loan be unsecured only as long as all the other major creditors of this borrower are going to be in the same boat. If somebody else tries to jump ahead and get secured, this lender will also be secured—or there will be a default under the loan agreement.

It's also typical to include a term that says that the company can't have other agreements that contain restrictions on liens (other than, of course, the lender's own loan agreement here). The lender does not want the restriction on liens in this agreement to trigger a default under any of the company's other agreements—nor, usually, does the company.

Investments and Acquisitions

The company will usually be restricted from investing its cash in other companies, whether via making a loan or making an equity investment. The company will also be restricted from making acquisitions. As usual, there will be a few exceptions to these limitations.

First, there will typically be a list of existing investments that the company can continue to maintain, and this will appear on a schedule at the back of the agreement. Second, the company will usually be allowed to own "cash equivalents," which are defined as treasury bonds or other highly rated securities. Intercompany investments will be permitted, as mentioned in the debt covenant section, and will be uncapped if all the subsidiaries are guarantors of the loan, and subject to a cap if the subsidiaries are not guarantors. The company may also be permitted to acquire securities or other non-cash consideration in exchange for settling an obligation owed to it, or as partial payment for an asset sale.

The company might also be permitted to do acquisitions within certain guidelines, but this is typically reserved for larger companies with strong financial results. If the company is permitted to make acquisitions without prior consent from the lender, the acquisitions usually have to fit within a dollar limit as to the purchase price. Also, the acquisition usually can't be a hostile takeover, can't result in a breach of any other term of the loan agreement, must result in compliance with the financial covenants (calculated on a pro forma basis, as if the acquisition had taken place at the start of the accounting period), must include advance notice and certifications made to the lender, and a long list of other conditions must be met. Frequently, even when certain acquisitions are permitted, the company ends up needing to ask the lender for permission anyway, as one or more of these conditions will not be met.

Guarantees and Other Contingent Obligations

For this covenant to make any sense, you'll first have to look at the definition of "indebtedness" in your loan agreement to see if it includes guarantees and contingent liabilities or not. Many times, the debt covenant restricts not just debt, but contingent obligations as well. If it doesn't, there will be a separate provision relating to contingent obligations. Similar to the debt covenant, this covenant will prohibit all but a few common types of guarantees and contingent payments, including those in existence on the closing date, contingent obligations in connection with interest rate hedges (especially if hedging of the term loan is required in the affirmative covenants section), ordinary course guarantees of obligations of suppliers, franchisees and licensees, and perhaps additional guarantees or other obligations within a dollar cap.

Payment of Dividends and Subordinated Debt

A senior lender usually does not want other debt to be paid before its own loan is paid. Even more important, the lender will not want equity holders to be paid before its loan is paid. Why is this? Well, first of all, equity holders generally stand to receive a higher rate of return than debt holders. The ultimate value of the company belongs to them. Debt holders have the benefit of priority of repayment (even in a bankruptcy proceeding, debt holders are paid in full before the equity holders receive anything) so they usually have a lower rate of return, meaning that the interest rate on the debt is lower than the dividend rate a preferred stockholder would receive. Because of the priorities given under the bankruptcy code, there is a strong desire to keep the equity owners from taking anything out of the company or receiving any significant return on their investment while the debt is still unpaid and the lender's commitments remain in effect.

With this in mind, it is easier to understand why a lender would include covenants restricting payments of dividends and subordinated debt. These covenants are sometimes found under the heading "Restricted Junior Payments," as they all relate to payments of obligations that are junior in priority to the loan. The payments prohibited in this covenant will be dividends, repurchases of stock or stock redemptions, exercise of redemption rights under bond offerings, and prepayment of any subordinated debt from a junior creditor (though not payment at maturity, unless the subordinated lender has agreed to these restrictions in an intercreditor or subordination agreement). Payment of interest on other debt may be permitted— and indeed often is—though it depends on the nature of the deal.

If the borrower is a subsidiary of a holding company, the lender may permit some cash to be distributed up to the holding company for limited purposes. Payments for tax liabilities relating to the operations of the company, and for administrative costs and expenses that are attributable to the company, are usually permitted, as these may have been borne by the borrower itself absent the holding company's existence.

73

Fundamental Changes

The company will be required to agree not to change its corporate structure, or "merge, consolidate, liquidate, wind-up," or otherwise dissolve itself. It seems obvious why this would be important. The company needs to continue its existence during the term of the loan. That said, it's fairly common for an internal merger (between subsidiaries) or consolidation to be permitted as long as the company is the surviving entity from that merger. So, for example, the company could merge one of its subsidiaries into itself, and this would pose no problem at all. Acquiring a new company via merger would of course require the company to meet the terms of the other negative covenant that prohibits acquisitions, in addition to meeting the requirements of this covenant.

Asset Sales

I tend to get a lot of questions about asset sales. The company will be planning to get rid of some old equipment that it isn't using anymore, or will have an opportunity to sell a portion of its business for a good price. The question will be whether this can be done without lender consent—and if you do it, what do you have to do with the proceeds?

Here's the answer. First, take a look at the negative covenants in your loan agreement. The company is usually prohibited from disposing of assets, but (you guessed it) with a few exceptions. There will be an exception for sales of assets that are worth only small dollar amounts. And, there will usually be exceptions permitting disposal of obsolete, worn-out, or surplus property, and for discounting accounts receivable in the ordinary course of business (other than in an asset-based loan). Certainly, sales of inventory in the ordinary course of business will always be permitted.

The wording of the exceptions matters. Sometimes you will only be allowed to dispose of worn-out equipment, but not surplus equipment, or perhaps only equipment and not other types of assets. Doing anything that isn't expressly permitted will require consent from the lender. This is something to consider when negotiating the loan agreement. If you frequently dispose of certain kinds of items, you would want to bring this up and see whether the lender is willing to permit at least some of those dispositions up front, without your having to go back and ask for consent each time.

The other thing to be aware of when doing an asset sale is that it's common for an asset sale to be a trigger for a mandatory prepayment. Take a look at the mandatory prepayment section (back near the beginning of the agreement) to see if this is the case in your deal. Often there will be some kind of threshold established (i.e., you only have to prepay the loan if you receive more than $100,000 in any calendar year from permitted asset sales), so that not every dollar needs to be applied to prepay the loan. Also, check the timing, because some loan agreements require "immediate" prepayment, while others give you a few days to send in the money. This is often a negotiated point in the agreement.

Transactions with Affiliates

Usually, the loan agreement will include a covenant restricting dealings with shareholders and other affiliates. Unless the terms of those dealings are equivalent to what the company would get from a third party—also known as "arm's length" terms—the lender will want these types of deals to be prohibited. The lender won't want the company to be making sweetheart deals with its shareholders or officers, where they get paid more than they would otherwise get, since that would be another way for the equity owners or affiliates to get money out of the company sooner. (We already know that lenders don't like that idea.)

Exceptions to the rule here will include permission for the company to engage in transactions with its own subsidiaries or parent company (to the extent permitted elsewhere under the other covenants), payment of customary fees to board members for their service on the board of directors, reimbursement of customary costs and expenses of officers and employees, and other customary types of payments. There may also be a schedule listing existing arrangements that the lender will decide to approve as of the closing date.

For example, it is not unusual for a small company to lease its office space from one of its shareholders (or another company owned by the shareholder), and the lender will permit this to continue if the lease is favorable—or at least not unfavorable—to the company.

For companies owned by private equity sponsors, the lender may permit some management fees to be paid to the sponsor, and may permit costs and expenses to be reimbursed pursuant to the terms of an existing management agreement. The lender may wish to put a cap on the amount that can be paid, and may require that the company meet certain leverage tests before making management fee payments. This is in keeping with the principle that equity is paid after debt. Payment of management fees may be well-deserved, or may on occasion be viewed by the lender as a potential end-run around the restriction on payment of dividends.

Chapter 14

Defaults and Remedies

This part is hard, because no one wants to think that bad things might happen to them. Lawyers are trained to think about all the things that can go wrong and how the deal might go bad, so we can advise our clients on how to avoid all the potential bad outcomes. But I recognize that we're in the minority on this one. Most normal (non-lawyer) people don't start a new deal with the thought in mind that it's going to end badly. If they did, deals would never get done!

There's a relatively standard list of things that can constitute a "default" under a loan agreement.

Default vs. Event of Default

This is another question that comes up a lot. What's the difference between a "default" and an "event of default"? In plain English, these words would mean pretty much the same thing, but in legal terms there is a real difference. (See, here's yet another example of the bizarre way lawyers use language.) The simple answer is that a "default" is just an "event of default" waiting to happen. The non-simple answer is that a default is "a condition or event that, after notice or lapse of time or both, would constitute an event of default."

The default section of your loan agreement lists all the things that constitute an "event of default." We sometimes call these the "capital E" events of default (as in "Events of Default"), because the defined term is capitalized when it's used in the credit agreement. When one of these things happens, you are fully in default.

When a capital "D" default (a "Default") happens, as opposed to a full-blown Event of Default, you still might be restricted from doing certain things. This term is commonly used in the negative covenants section (for example, you might not be able to make acquisitions, if the acquisition covenant says you can only acquire a company "so long as there is no Default or Event of Default then in existence"). The prohibition is triggered on the earlier "potential" Default rather than full Event of Default. If you have a revolving line of credit, you usually will not be able to borrow funds if there is a Default.

Remember, though, that you aren't yet truly in default under the loan agreement until an Event of Default actually occurs, and the lenders can't yet seek remedies against you (more on this later).

Types of Defaults

Okay, now we're ready to move into the list of events of default.

Payment

The first item on the list is always "failure to pay." You'll be in default if you don't pay principal on time. You will also be in default if you don't pay interest, fees, or other types of payments on time—though it is customary in many types of loans to allow for a short grace period of a few days for late payments on these other (non-principal) types of payments.

Breach of Covenants

It will be an event of default under the loan agreement if the borrower breaches any of the covenants. This is not surprising, as it makes sense that both parties will be required to abide by the terms they've agreed to. It is fairly common to include a cure period as to some of the covenants (for example, failure to comply with an affirmative covenant might not trigger a default unless the failure continues for 30 days and is not cured by the borrower during that period). Cure periods usually won't apply to any of the negative covenants or to covenants that already have a period of time built in (i.e., if delivery of financial statements is required by the 45th day after the end of the fiscal quarter, the default will occur as of that date with no additional period of time provided).

Breach of Representations and Warranties

Similarly, if the lender later finds that a representation was false when made (or deemed made), that too will be a default. As mentioned previously, representations don't necessarily have to be true all of the time. Only an inaccuracy at the time the representations are made will generate a default under the loan agreement. Note also that this default usually isn't limited to the representations stated in the "Representations and Warranties" section of the loan agreement. Representations made in certificates, guarantees, security agreements, or other loan documents can also create a default here, if they were false when made. Note that it's common to include a materiality qualifier here, so that the default is stated as failure of the representation to be true and correct "in any material respect" when made, so that immaterial misstatements don't bring down the whole house of cards.

Breach of Other Agreements: Cross-Default

The cross-default provision may be the most heavily negotiated event of default. What it says is that a default under another loan, in and of itself, will cause an automatic default under this loan, too.

The borrower will want to negotiate this provision so that it doesn't apply to every kind of debt or to every kind of default that might occur under that debt. At a minimum, the borrower will want to have some kind of threshold amount set (i.e., "only debt in excess of $250,000 in principal amount") so that small items we don't even really think of as debt or that could very easily be paid off don't trigger a default.

A payment default under other debt will always constitute a default under this loan, but other types of defaults (breaches of covenants, etc.) usually don't trigger the cross-default provision unless the defaults cause or permit the holder of that debt to accelerate it (declare it due before its stated maturity). Very large, highly rated companies can negotiate for cross-acceleration here—where the cross-default doesn't happen unless the other loan actually is accelerated (not just "permitted" to be accelerated). Cross-acceleration is also often used in junior or subordinated loans.

Default Under Other Loan Documents

The loan agreement is probably not the only document you'll have to sign in connection with this deal. There might be a separate security agreement (more on this later), promissory notes, guarantees, mortgages or deeds of trust, officer's certificates, and all sorts of other things. Since all of these documents relate to the same deal, it would be difficult for all the parties (and would create confusion) if you could have a default under the note or under the security agreement that wasn't also a default under the loan agreement—or vice versa. So, somewhere in the events of default section there will be a provision saying that any default under any of the other loan documents is also a default under the loan agreement.

Loan Documents Invalid, Security Interest Failure, Etc.

It will be an event of default if any of the loan documents ceases to be in effect after the closing (for example, if it is declared void by a court for some reason), if the lenders fail to have a valid and perfected lien on the collateral, or if the borrower contests the validity or enforceability of the loan documents. This provision is meant to protect against unexpected things that can happen in legal proceedings.

When we sign the loan agreement, we all expect that the terms in it are valid and enforceable. We also expect the security interests granted to the lender to be valid and enforceable. But if a court says otherwise—or if the borrower itself tries to get a court to say otherwise—all bets are off. Of course, practically speaking, if a court decides that the entire loan agreement is void, then being able to declare a default under that void agreement is pretty useless. This provision is more likely to be useful if only a particular part of the agreement is declared void. The rest of the agreement would continue to be in effect—including this default provision, which would allow the lender to seek remedies in order to protect itself in its newly compromised position.

Bankruptcy

Obviously, if the company files for bankruptcy, that's going to be extremely significant to the lender. That being true, credit agreements always establish that a bankruptcy filing is a default.

Since it's possible for three of the company's creditors to get together and file an involuntary bankruptcy proceeding against the company, an involuntary case is usually only a default if it continues for more than a reasonable period of time—usually something like 60 days—and is not dismissed by the court.

The filing of a voluntary bankruptcy case (initiated by the company itself), by contrast, is an immediate default with no cure period. Likewise, the actual insolvency of the company, or approval of the board of directors to file a bankruptcy case, will also be an immediate default.

If a bankruptcy proceeding does get underway with respect to the borrower, the remedies section of the credit agreement will usually provide that the loan is automatically accelerated, simultaneous with the bankruptcy filing. This means the entire loan is considered due and payable in full as of that time. Absent unusual circumstances, the bankruptcy code will automatically provide for this anyway. This way, the lender can make a claim for the full amount of the loan and not just whatever happened to be due at the time of the filing. And, the lender making that claim won't violate the automatic stay that otherwise goes into effect to prevent actions against the borrower during bankruptcy proceedings.

A question that sometimes comes up here is whether bankruptcy of the company's subsidiaries should also trigger a default.

Sometimes borrowers negotiate to remove the default for immaterial or non-operating subsidiaries, but subsidiaries that are guarantors of the loan are usually not permitted to be excluded.

Dissolution

As explained previously, if the company ceases to exist, that's obviously going to create a problem for the lender. (This falls into the "Well, duh!" category of terms.) The default will be stated fairly broadly, and will include any judgment, order, or decree for the dissolution or windup of the borrower being entered by a court—not just the actual dissolution or windup itself.

ERISA Events

Employee benefit plans and ERISA issues show up again here, too. A material liability under an ERISA benefit plan (especially unfunded pension plan liability) or a violation of ERISA would constitute a default under the loan agreement. Sometimes there is discussion about just how "material" the event has to be. Setting a dollar amount for this is helpful.

Change of Control

It will be a default if the company is no longer majority owned by the people (or entities) who owned it on the closing date. Sometimes this appears in the covenants section, and sometimes it is an event of default. I think as a matter of proper drafting, it belongs in the default section. The borrower is not in a position to control its shareholders or to tell them whether or not to dispose of their stock, so requiring them to do so in the covenant section seems a bit inappropriate. Regardless, if the stockholders do decide to sell their equity interests in the company, the occurrence of that event can be a default (there's nothing here about anybody having to do anything; it's just an objective question about whether the event happened or not).

How a change of control is defined will vary from deal to deal. It is often defined as the existing shareholders failing to continue to hold at least a majority of the outstanding voting shares. Sometimes it is important that a particular individual or group of individuals continue to hold all of the shares that they hold today, and if that's the case, the requirement will be set more tightly. For public companies, the requirement will be stated in the reverse; it will be triggered if anyone who doesn't have a controlling interest today obtains such an interest in the future. Control can be defined as 20% of the voting stock, or 30%, or more—whatever is agreed.

Remedies

It is very important to understand what the consequences are when you go into default under your loan agreement. Be sure to talk to your attorney about this, so that you really understand what can happen. The consequences of a default can be very severe, including foreclosure on all your assets. That said, it can also be true that a default doesn't result in the lender exercising any remedies at all. It really depends on the circumstances at the time, and whether the default indicates a potentially serious problem or just a minor hiccup.

Some "Early" Remedies

As an initial matter, a default can (and often does) trigger a higher interest rate. This is usually stated in the interest rate section at the front of the agreement. Depending on what it says, the lender might be permitted to charge default interest as soon as any kind of default occurs, or there might have to be a payment default. Default interest rates are high and can result in a significantly higher cost to you over time. If your interest rate was based on LIBOR, the lender will probably also have the right to switch to the Base Rate (or Prime Rate) as the basis for calculating your interest rate.

The lender can also cut off additional funding. This isn't an issue with a term loan (since it was already funded in full, up front), but if you have a revolving line of credit that you regularly draw on, this can be a significant consequence for you as well.

The lender will also have the right to require you to cash collateralize any letters of credit that are outstanding. This means you have to give the lender enough cash to cover its liabilities on the letters of credit (and often a small cushion, 105% or 110% of the face amount of the letters of credit), which it will hold in an account and use to repay itself if the letters of credit are drawn on by the beneficiary.

These are remedies that are fairly quick and easy for the lender to impose. As such, they are fairly frequently used by lenders—or threatened to be used. They may apply only temporarily, until you get things sorted out with the lender, or they may apply for a long period of time.

Full Remedies

If the default is relatively minor, the lender usually doesn't jump immediately into exercising all the remedies that are available to it. Most of the time, the lender will want more information from the borrower about what's going on at the company and what led to the default, so it can make a determination about how severe the problem is and how best to proceed.

If it looks like things can be worked out, the lender will usually attempt to negotiate a solution with the borrower. Sometimes the lender will agree to waive the defaults in exchange for some additional restrictions on the company's operations (elimination of some baskets from the negative covenants, for example) along with payment of an amendment fee or a higher rate of interest.

It is important to understand that the lender has the right to take drastic remedies against the company if it chooses to do so. The lender has to act in good faith, in accordance with principles of "good faith and fair dealing," but seeking remedies may be well within those principles, depending on the circumstances.

The lender will have the right to exercise remedies available to it by law, and, in addition, may specifically negotiate terms in the loan agreement providing certain additional things it can do, including:

>> accelerate the loan, so that the entire amount outstanding (plus accrued interest, fees, expenses, etc.) is immediately due and payable in full,

>> terminate all obligations to loan money or issue letters of credit, and

>> take steps to exercise rights against the collateral, including foreclosure and sale of all of your assets that are subject to the security interest.

Foreclosure or Bankruptcy

If things have deteriorated to the point where the lender is looking to seize your assets, you might consider filing for bankruptcy protection. These options should be carefully weighed, with advice of counsel.

For some companies, it makes more sense to try for a sale outside of bankruptcy, as bankruptcy is an expensive and lengthy process. This is something the lender and borrower might discuss and consider together.

The lender also has the right to conduct an "Article 9" asset sale (of personal property, but not real property) under the provisions of Article 9 of the Uniform Commercial Code. This would result in a sale of the assets to the highest bidder. If it's a public sale (like an auction), the lender can credit bid, which means the lender can enter bids in amounts up to the total amount of money the borrower owes it under the loan, and thereby acquire the assets itself without paying cash. For real property, the lender can undertake a judicial foreclosure or other procedure permitted by state law.

Usually the lender isn't really interested in owning the assets of the business. The lender isn't engaged in manufacturing toys or chartering airplanes (or whatever your business does); it is in the business of dealing with money. So the lender will want to sell the assets to someone else for as high a price as possible, to maximize repayment of the loan.

There are many different ways that a default situation can turn out. I've mentioned a few of them here because sometimes it helps to understand what can happen if things go wrong. We'll just hope that this remains nothing more than a mildly interesting academic exercise for you, and that you never have the opportunity to obtain practical experience with any of these things.

Chapter 15

Amendments

Being able to amend the credit agreement is so important that I want to devote a whole chapter to it. Since loan agreements are long-term arrangements, you might easily find yourself amending your loan agreement, or seeking lender consent for something you want to do, seven, eight, or even ten times during the term of the loan. It's impossible to predict all the things that will happen to your business over a period of years, so it's to be expected that changes will be necessary.

If you get to a point where there have been a lot of amendments, you might prefer to just "amend and restate" the agreement in its entirety, so you can read it more easily. It becomes nearly impossible to work through the contents of ten amendments each time you need to figure out exactly what the agreement says!

Why Are Amendments Necessary?

The company will be interested in being able to get amendments (or waivers) as easily as possible. This is for several reasons. First, you might find errors in the agreement that need to be fixed. Sometimes there's an odd typo here or there. If it's something that creates confusion, like "the interest rate margin effective as of the closing date shall be two percent (4%) per annum" (which leaves everyone wondering whether it's supposed to be two or four), it ought to be corrected. You'd be surprised how often things like this happen.

You might also discover after the closing that some of the covenants just don't work for your company. For example, maybe you have a joint venture that you are obligated to make certain minimum contributions to over the next few years. The contributions you make are in the form of licenses to use technology, not cash. Because no money was involved, you had forgotten about this when negotiating your loan agreement. The language of the negative covenant prohibiting asset sales (and other dispositions of assets, which these licenses are) is not broad enough to permit this technology licensing. So, you'll need an amendment to the loan agreement—or an express waiver of that covenant—in order to continue to comply with the terms of your joint venture agreement.

You might also need amendments because your circumstances change over time. This is probably the most common reason for needing an amendment. It could be a positive change—like the opportunity to make an acquisition or open a new location that will expand your business. Or it could be that your business is suffering a bit during an economic downturn, or because of problems in your industry, and perhaps you need some temporary relief from having to meet financial covenants. If you are in default, the agreement may need to be amended as part of the loan workout process, with some of the amendments being required by the lenders as described previously.

Timing becomes absolutely critical if the company gets into any financial trouble. Companies in trouble often need temporary waivers of their financial covenants—and possibly other covenants as well—in order to continue in business and not live with the threat of lender action on a default.

If you have a loan from a single lender, getting an amendment may not be too difficult. At the other end of the spectrum, with a large syndicated credit facility, it can be very hard to get the lenders in a diverse bank group to agree to provide an amendment. This is where majority voting becomes really important, because it means you can go ahead with the amendment even though you have a few holdouts among the banks.

Who Has to Agree to the Amendment?

An agreement is amended by the parties to the agreement. So, for a loan, the lender and the borrower would need to agree on the amended terms and sign an amendment to the loan agreement in order to change the loan terms.

In a syndicated loan, with multiple lenders, the amendment process can be much more complicated.

If you have a syndicated loan, you will want most of the provisions of that loan to be capable of being amended with a majority vote of the lenders. Whenever more than a majority vote is required, it's just going to be that much harder to get changes made when you need them. This is an issue that's important to both the borrower and the lenders.

Some credit agreements will require class voting—where a majority vote of each affected "class" of lenders needs to be obtained. For example, a majority of the lenders who have commitments under the revolving loan, plus, separately, a majority of the lenders with term loans outstanding, will need to vote. Other agreements have certain terms that require "supermajority" votes—so, for example, a vote of 66% is required in order to approve a change to the negative covenant prohibiting the company from taking on additional subordinated debt, but not for other covenants. This would happen if some of the lenders were concerned about this issue in this particular case and negotiated for this requirement.

Some amendments will require not just a supermajority, but 100% of the lenders to vote for the change. There is a fairly typical list of these issues that tend to come up over and over again in loan agreements. It used to be that loan agreements would just list these things as requiring the vote of "all Lenders." Today, it is more common to say "all Lenders directly affected thereby" so as to eliminate the need for a vote from a lender whose loan isn't affected by the change. The types of amendments usually requiring this "100%" lender vote include:

>> reducing the principal amount of the lender's loan,

89

>> postponing the scheduled maturity date of the loan or extending the termination date applicable to a revolving line of credit,

>> postponing the date or reducing the amount of any scheduled amortization payment (but not prepayment) of principal,

>> postponing the date on which any interest or fees are payable,

>> decreasing (but not increasing) the interest rate applicable to the loan,

>> reducing the amount or postponing the due date of any other amounts payable under the loan agreement (for example, payments with respect to letters of credit, or prepayment events),

>> extending the expiration date of any letter of credit beyond the maturity date for the revolving line of credit,

>> amending the definition of Pro Rata Share or any of the pro rata sharing provisions, to provide for other than strict "pro rata" sharing of payments among the lenders,

>> amending the definition of Required Lenders or any of the voting provisions,

>> releasing liens on all or substantially all of the collateral (or, in some deals, a material amount of the collateral), or

>> releasing all or substantially all of the guarantors (or any material guarantor) from their guarantees.

In addition, the vote of any lender who issues letters of credit under the facility will be required to change the letter of credit provisions; similarly, if you have a swingline loan (see Chapter 5 for a description of this type of loan), the vote of the swingline lender will be required to amend provisions relating to swingline loans, and the vote of the administrative agent will be required as to matters relating specifically to the agent.

A Note About How the Vote Is Calculated

We should note that lender votes are counted based on the dollar amount of each lender's commitment and/or outstanding loans, not based on the number of lenders. It's never a one-lender, one-vote situation.

Let's consider an example with a revolving line of credit. To determine whether we've received a majority vote, we need to figure out how much each lender has committed to provide under the revolving credit facility. The total amount of the facility equals 100% of the lender commitments. If we have five lenders who each have committed 20% of the facility, we need three lenders (holding collectively 60% of the commitments, in this case) to vote in favor of the amendment in order to have a vote of a majority of the commitments. What if there aren't just unused commitments but also revolving loans outstanding at the time? We can still calculate the vote based on commitments to lend—whether the commitments are used or unused at that time.

For term loans, once the loans are funded, there is no issue as to used or unused commitments. We can look at either the commitment amount of each lender or the principal amount of the loans outstanding, and in either case we should come up with the same relative percentage held by each lender. This is because the loan must be repaid on a pro rata (equal) basis among the lenders, in accordance with their percentages. Let's say we have a $10 million loan with three lenders, where the first lender has loaned 50% of the total amount, and the other two lenders have each loaned 25% of the total. If the borrower pays back $1 million of this loan, the first lender will receive half of that payment, or $500,000, and the other two lenders will each receive $250,000. Each of the lenders continues to hold the very same percentage as before—50/25/25—though as to a lesser total principal amount now. Some loan agreements permit the term loan lenders to waive the right to receive prepayments. If only some of the lenders (but not all) were to waive receipt of a payment, the lenders' pro rata shares would need to be recalculated to reflect this.

These things can become important if there is disagreement among the lenders. Sometimes it comes down to just a few dollars in commitment amounts that make all the difference in getting the vote needed to adopt the amendment.

Chapter 16

Boilerplate: Assignments, Confidentiality, Etc.

Now we get into some of the "boilerplate" provisions in the loan agreement.

I can't tell you how many times I've heard people say, "Oh, that stuff at the back is all just boilerplate anyway, so why should I look at it?" And if you have hired good counsel, maybe you're right, and you don't need to look too closely at it yourself—as long as your counsel is looking at it and letting you know what's important.

In some sense, it's true. There is a bunch of stuff at the back of the agreement that rarely changes from loan agreement to loan agreement. We will have the same language in there about rights of setoff, about headings not having any meaning, about the document being governed by New York law, and so on. But, some sections are negotiated and should be reviewed a bit more carefully, as there can be traps hidden in the so-called "standard" language.

Assignments and Participations

Somewhere in this back section of the loan agreement, there will be a provision permitting the lender (but never the borrower) to assign the loan to someone else. In a syndicated loan, where some of the lenders likely intend to sell off portions of the loan to other financial institutions rather quickly after closing, these terms might get negotiated a bit among the lenders themselves. The borrower will want to look closely at these provisions to make sure it isn't taking on obligations to new parties without adequate protection of its interests.

First, let's understand what an assignment is, as opposed to a participation. An assignment of the loan removes the existing lender from the transaction and substitutes another lender in its place, fully and completely. The borrower will usually want the right to consent to an assignment, and it is customary for this to be permitted as long as the borrower is not in default (but once you're in default, all bets are off). There has been some movement in the market toward eliminating the borrower's right to consent to assignments, and there is some pressure to do this so that lenders can more easily dispose of entire portfolios of loans when they are getting out of the lending business or need to clean up their balance sheets. There is still quite a bit of resistance to this concept among borrowers, however. In addition to borrower consent, assignments usually are subject to some basic requirements, such as that the assignee be an appropriate financial institution that is adequately capitalized, that the agent consent to the transaction and receive a fee, and that the assignment be for at least a reasonable minimum amount. Some borrowers also negotiate for other limitations, such as no assignments (or participations) to competitors of the borrower.

A participation can take several forms, but for our purposes here it is sufficient to think of it as a behind-the-scenes deal between lenders. The lender remains the "lender" under the loan agreement and deals directly with the borrower and agent as usual. Behind the scenes, the lender sells participations to other lending institutions, who do not become parties to the loan agreement with the borrower. They are parties to a separate participation agreement only among themselves, and the participant lenders do not have any direct rights against the borrower. Indeed, the borrower is likely to be unaware of any participations and will not have the right to consent to them. The participants share in the loan risk (in one form or another—funding risk, repayment risk, or both) that the original lender had. There are standard forms used for loan participations among lenders. The borrower's biggest concern here will be to make sure that it is not taking on obligations to the participants.

Participants are usually permitted to have the benefits of increased costs, capital adequacy, and break-funding provisions of the loan agreement (see below) to the same extent that the primary lender is entitled to receive those payments, but are only entitled to the benefit of tax provisions in the agreement if they also provide all the required tax withholding forms to the borrower. These are all issues for negotiation, and the wording is important.

Expense Reimbursement

It is standard for all expenses related to the loan to be the borrower's responsibility. Sometimes borrowers are a bit concerned about this, but it is absolutely customary in the corporate lending world for the lender's costs—including the fees of its legal counsel—to be paid for by the borrower. This is one of those things that is typically non-negotiable, as the lender usually is not charging enough in fees or interest to cover these out-of-pocket costs and still have its lending operations be profitable.

It is appropriate for the borrower to pay "reasonable" costs and expenses of preparing the loan documents, including any amendments and waivers. Lender costs can include things like appraisals, travel expenses for visiting your offices or conducting site inspections, title insurance fees, filing and recording fees, and other similar things.

In a syndicated loan, the borrower normally pays only the costs and expenses of the administrative agent, not all the lenders. If the other lenders have any costs or expenses, they are likely to be minimal and are not reimbursed. This is true until the loan goes into default and the lenders are seeking to enforce their rights. In enforcement actions, all costs and expenses of all lenders are to be borne by the borrower. There is usually relatively little negotiation of cost reimbursement provisions, and the negotiation will focus on things like use of the term "reasonable" to qualify which types of expenses are reimbursed, and perhaps whether the fees of more than one outside counsel can be reimbursed.

Taxes, Break-Funding Costs, Capital Adequacy

These provisions can appear up front in the section of the agreement relating to loan payments, or they can appear here in the back. In any case, the loan agreement will say somewhere that if tax withholding is required based on payments that the borrower owes to the lender under the agreement, the borrower will be required to make the withholding, but then "gross up" the payments it makes to the lender so that the lender will receive the same amount as always, as if there were no withholding. The lender is required to send the borrower all of the legally required forms relating to tax withholding, so that exemptions from withholding can be established (and no gross-up will apply). In the United States, there will be no tax issues for interest paid on a bank loan if the proper forms are completed to document the nature of the transaction. With most foreign lenders, there are tax treaties and other laws that eliminate tax withholding issues, but you can't count on this always being the case. As with anything tax related, get good advice from qualified professionals before doing anything.

If the loan bears interest at a rate based on LIBOR, there will also be provisions requiring the borrower to pay any costs the lender incurs if the borrower pays back the loan on a date other than the last day of the applicable interest period. These costs are called break-funding costs.

Similarly, if the lender is subjected to additional capital adequacy requirements by banking regulators in connection with its loan to the borrower, the borrower will need to compensate the lender for its additional costs.

Indemnification

Similar to cost reimbursement, the loan agreement will require the borrower to reimburse the lender for any and all losses related to the loan. What's intended here is that if the lender is sued by someone else because of this loan, the cost will be borne by the borrower, including any amounts that have to be paid as a judgment in the case.

This applies to any kind of case. Let's take the example of an environmental problem. Assume there's some environmental contamination discovered on the borrower's property, and it spreads to the neighboring properties. The neighbors believe they've suffered losses as a result of this contamination, and they bring a lawsuit. Because the lenders have mortgages on the borrower's property, the neighbors can name the lenders as defendants in the case, along with the borrower. All the costs the lenders end up incurring for this litigation (hiring attorneys to prepare the defense, expert witnesses, etc.) will be passed on to the borrower. In addition, if a judgment is entered against the lenders, this amount will also be payable by the borrower under the indemnification terms in the loan agreement.

Indemnification provisions can sometimes be negotiated in relatively small ways, but the lender is likely to resist significant wording changes since much of the language in this section is often required as a matter of policy within the lending institution.

Set-Off Rights

Though the law provides some limitations on this, the lenders will want to have established the right to "set off" any amounts they have on deposit against the loan amounts that the borrower owes them. This is one of those things that needs to be specifically stated in the loan agreement, so that under state law (depending on which state you're in), if there is a default, the lender will be able to take the borrower's cash held in deposit accounts at its own institution and apply the cash to repay the loan. Often, a deposit account control agreement will give the lender this right anyway, but those agreements usually apply to accounts held at other (non-lender) institutions. This provision in the loan agreement is intended to get the lender into the same position with accounts held at its own institution.

Pro Rata Sharing

Somewhere in the loan agreement, whether earlier or here at the back, if there is more than one lender in the deal, there will be a term requiring that the lenders share "ratably" in any payments received from the borrower. This means that each lender shares in the payment in proportion to the dollar amount of the loans that it made (or the commitments that it has; presumably these are one and the same). As in our prior example, if there are three lenders, and one of them loaned half the money while the other two each loaned one-fourth, this term in the agreement basically says that each time a payment comes in from the borrower, the money is split up so that half goes to the first lender and one-fourth goes to each of the other two lenders. Ratable sharing of payments ensures that the lenders are paid back at the same rate and one doesn't somehow get ahead of the others. This term also applies to "payments" received as a result of exercising set-off rights (described above) and to any amounts collected as a result of enforcement actions against the borrower.

Confidentiality

Confidentiality provisions are often negotiated. Indeed you might find that the lender doesn't include a confidentiality provision at all until you ask for it. You'll want to make sure the company's information is kept confidential except under certain limited circumstances.

Exceptions to the requirement that the lender keep your information confidential will include things like disclosures

>> to the lender's accountants, attorneys, and agents, so long as they also are instructed to keep the information confidential,

>> to government or regulatory agencies who request the information,

>> if required by law or by subpoenas or other legal processes,

>> in connection with the exercise of remedies against the borrower, or in lawsuits relating to the loan agreement itself,

>> to prospective assignees or participants of the loans, so long as they agree to maintain confidentiality,

>> if the borrower consents to the disclosure (no surprise there), or

>> if the information becomes publicly available, or available to the lender on a non-confidential basis from another source, other than due to improper disclosure by the lender or anyone else who is subject to a confidentiality agreement.

Sometimes there will be negotiation about whether the lender needs to notify the company of any intended disclosure (for example, if served with a subpoena). Lenders also like to be able to disclose the existence of the loan agreement to service providers who collect data about the market, so that they can be properly ranked in the tables as the lender having the most loans in the mining industry, or whatever it is. The lender might also want permission to mention this loan in advertisements that it makes about its lending capabilities, and such advertisements would typically include limited information such as the name of the borrower and the amount (and type) of the loan made. The lender might also ask that you mark anything that's confidential as "Confidential" so that there is no doubt as to which items need to be held in confidence. With privately owned companies, there isn't usually a requirement to mark items as "Confidential" since all of the company's information should be considered confidential (there are no public filings, after all).

Jury Trial Waiver

For a variety of reasons, most banks assume that they will not fare well in a trial by jury. So, the lender is likely to want the borrower to expressly waive its right to a trial by jury. The alternatives to trial by jury include trial by the judge or binding arbitration outside of the court process, either of which may be provided for in your loan agreement.

In California, where pre-dispute jury trial waivers are understood to be unenforceable, provisions for arbitration or "judicial reference" (a special dispute resolution procedure that is similar to arbitration) will appear in this spot in your loan agreement, rather than a waiver.

Governing Law

The parties to the agreement get to decide which state law will be used to interpret the meaning of the terms. The idea is that if you ever end up in court—wherever you are—you want to know ahead of time how the terms will be viewed by the court, and what the court will say they mean.

A lot of corporate loan agreements are governed by New York law. This is true regardless of what state you're in, and sometimes regardless of what state the lender is in. New York has a very well-established set of banking laws (and court cases interpreting those laws), and it tends to be a "lender-friendly" state. This makes it an attractive choice of law for lenders, certainly, but also for some borrowers because there is some additional certainty of outcome in a jurisdiction with this much banking history.

I live in California, which tends to be at the opposite end of the spectrum when it comes to lending matters. California is widely viewed as a "borrower-friendly" state, with many statutory protections established in state law for the benefit of borrowers and guarantors of loans. Though several of these statutory protections can be waived, there are many lenders who would still prefer to pick a different state law to govern their loan documents.

Consent to Jurisdiction

Similar to the governing law issue, the lender will want to establish that it can sue the borrower in a state that is convenient for it. If the lender's primary offices are in New York and the borrower is in Idaho, the lender will want the borrower to agree to be subject to the jurisdiction of a New York court. This is not just for convenience (it's expensive and time-consuming to travel for litigation—and note that these costs are often supposed to be paid by the borrower under the terms of the loan agreement), but it is common when New York law is chosen as the governing law, to help ensure consistent interpretation of the loan terms. Even though an Idaho court is supposed to apply New York law to the terms, an Idaho judge can't reasonably be expected to be familiar with New York law, and you won't have the same level of predictability as to the interpretation.

This part of the loan agreement is necessary because, unless you already have offices in New York yourself, you would be free to argue that a New York court doesn't have jurisdiction over your company (since you're not there, after all).

One important distinction to make is whether you are submitting to the "exclusive" jurisdiction of New York courts (meaning New York is the only place where the suit can be brought), or whether jurisdiction is "non-exclusive" (meaning you can always sue in New York but you don't have to; you can sue and be sued in other jurisdictions where the borrower or lender is located). You might think that none of this is important, because you don't expect to sue anyone or be sued, but you'd be surprised how significant these provisions are if the day ever does come.

No Waiver; Remedies Cumulative

As we've seen, lenders sometimes don't immediately take action if there's a default under the loan agreement. Really, they rarely take action immediately. Time goes by, discussions are had, things are done, and finally maybe the situation is resolved or something else happens. The "no waiver" provision in the loan agreement basically says that even though the lender has delayed taking action, or has taken no action, with respect to a default, that doesn't mean the lender has waived the default, and it doesn't mean the action will be accepted in the future. This is often coupled with a sentence or two saying that "all remedies are cumulative" and not exclusive—so that the lender remains entitled to the maximum remedies that would be available to it under the law in addition to all the remedies

101

specifically listed in the loan documents. In many cases, these provisions facilitate workouts and allow the borrower to take more time to correct problems, because the lender does not feel obligated to take immediate action whenever there is a default.

Independence of Covenants

If you're a lender, this is a handy provision to have around. What this says is that all the covenants are given independent effect, and it means that just because something appears to be permitted under one covenant in the agreement doesn't mean it is permitted everywhere. If another covenant somewhere else says you can't do it, then you can't do it—and you can't point back to the one covenant where it says it's okay and get away with it. This is helpful for lenders, but it makes for a lot of work for borrowers (really, for their counsel) who have to comb carefully through the loan agreement and make sure cross-references are included in each covenant, so that one covenant doesn't inadvertently take away what another covenant gave.

Survival of Representations

This term says that the representations survive execution and delivery of the agreement and the making of the loans. This is in response to an ancient legal doctrine that isn't worth describing here in any detail, but suffice to say there used to be a principle that once you signed the agreement and closed the deal, it was done and whatever was in it expired. This could hardly be true in a loan agreement that's intended to evidence an ongoing relationship, but we still include this sentence just in case.

Note that this does not mean that the representations are being made at any future date—unless you agreed to that in the representations and warranties section. This is a rather subtle distinction, but it just means that the representations still continue to "exist" such that the lender can sue you later if it turns out the representations were false at the time they were actually made by you (at the closing or on a later borrowing date).

Severability

A severability provision simply says that if any one part of the loan agreement turns out to be illegal, invalid, or unenforceable, the rest of the agreement will still stand. A problem in one part of the document doesn't void the entire thing.

Counterparts

The loan can be "executed in counterparts," which is a legalistic way of saying that the borrower can print out a copy of the loan agreement and sign it, and the lender can separately print out another copy of the agreement and sign on a different piece of paper. We don't both have to sign the very same page. It used to be a fun experience at the end of a deal to get together in a room for "The Signing" of all the loan documents. Hardly anybody does that anymore. We just sign separately and e-mail "pdf" copies of the signature pages to each other. It is possible to work on a large loan transaction for several weeks and get all the way through to closing without ever meeting anyone else face to face.

SYNDICATION

*The best part about being with a group is that
you don't have to do everything alone.*

~ Justin Timberlake

PART 3

Chapter 17

What Is Syndication?

Your lender wants to syndicate the loan. What does that mean for you?

Well, this usually means that you'll be able to get more money! Lenders syndicate loans for a variety of reasons, but usually it's because the loan amount exceeds the amount that the primary lender is able to hold on its own books. The hold level may have nothing to do with your business in particular. It might be due to regulatory restraints or having too much exposure to a single industry throughout the bank as a whole. To reach the desired hold level, the lender will syndicate the loan by bringing in other lenders.

In a syndicated loan, you'll have one primary lender who serves as the administrative agent. The administrative agent is initially selected by the borrower, and may be the lender you have the strongest relationship with or the one you feel the most confident about having in this role. The administrative agent will basically run the show for the group of lenders, taking the lead in working with the borrower to negotiate the loan documents and deal with issues that come up. This makes life a lot easier for the borrower, as it means you can just deal directly with the agent on most things, rather than working with 50 lenders separately.

The agent will work hard during the period before the loan closes to "syndicate" the credit facility. The process of syndication is a bit like underwriting a securities offering. The agent's syndications group (sometimes referred to as the "book runner" or "lead arranger") will contact people they know at other lending institutions who might be interested in this loan. They'll tell the lenders a bit about the company and the proposed loan transaction—a sales pitch, really. The agent will send each of the prospective lenders a confidential information memorandum, which includes specific information about the company and its operations, along with a term sheet for the loan. There may also be a bank meeting where the company's executives will give a presentation to the prospective lenders, sort of like a road show for securities. Any lender who receives confidential information about the company will be required to agree to non-disclosure terms first.

Some deals are widely syndicated, meaning that there will be many lenders in the deal. (One deal I worked on had more than 200 lenders in the group!) Still, it isn't unusual for a deal to be syndicated to a small group of four or five lenders. In any case, the agent will approach more lenders than it needs to fully syndicate the transaction, in case some of the lenders are unable to participate or aren't interested.

If the other lenders are interested in the deal, they'll let the agent know, and then they'll seek credit approval internally so they can be ready to make the loan on the closing date. Toward the end of the process, the agent will ask each lender to send in a commitment letter, indicating how much money they will commit to the loan, and whether they will loan under the revolving line of credit, term loan, or both (if more than one loan is being made).

If the lenders send in commitment letters committing to fund more than the expected size of the credit facility (more than the borrower needs or wants to borrow), the deal is "over-subscribed." In that case, the agent has the right to allocate the actual loan amount among the interested lenders in whatever way it wants. The agent might allocate the loan amount proportionately among the interested lenders, based on the amount each of them had delivered commitments for, but sometimes the agent will use this as an opportunity to reward lenders that have participated in other loans it syndicated recently, by giving those lenders a larger portion of this loan. The agent usually discusses with the borrower what its plans are for allocating the loan, so that relationships the borrower has (or doesn't have) with certain lenders can also be taken into account.

If not enough commitments are received, there are several options to consider. The borrower may choose to proceed with the loan at a smaller size. The agent and/or one or more of the other lenders may choose to increase their commitments to fill the gap. Or, the syndication process may be extended to see if other commitments will be received. Often there are a few lenders who indicate that they want to make a commitment but will need more time to get through their credit approval processes. In that case, choosing to wait a few days may mean you can receive the entire loan in the amount you originally wanted. Not surprisingly, around the holidays in December, and again in August when many bankers are on vacation, you may need to give lenders some additional time.

On the closing date, the borrower works directly with the agent to meet all of the closing conditions. The agent will send copies of the principal loan documents to the other lenders, both in draft form before the closing (so they can review and approve them), and in final signed form after the closing (for their records). If the lenders have questions or concerns about the loan documents, they will address those to the agent. The agent will deal with some of the issues on its own, or come back for input from the borrower. Again, this is much easier for the borrower than dealing with each of the lenders on its own, as the agent will be able to filter a lot of the questions.

The agent will deliver notices and documents to the lenders through a Web-based service such as IntraLinks or SyndTrak that is specifically designed for transactions of this type. Using one of these websites is handy because it means all of the documents will be together in one place, quickly accessible to everyone who is working on the transaction, but protected from being viewed by others. The service sends an e-mail alert to the entire working group every time something new is posted on the site. Ongoing deliveries of financial statements and other reports can be handled through the website, as can assignments of the loans to new lenders.

Chapter 18

The Agent's Role

During the term of the loan, the agent will handle all the funding of loans and payments to the lenders. If you are receiving a loan, on the funding day you'll get a single wire of money from the agent for the entire loan amount. Behind the scenes, the agent will have sent notices to all of the lenders and will have received funds from each of them according to their percentage of the total loan amount. The agent will then have aggregated the funds together for a single wire for you. Sometimes the agent will agree to fund loans to you prior to receiving funds from the lenders, to permit you to receive the funds a little faster than you might otherwise. In this case, the agent will look to each of the lenders to reimburse it for the lender's share of the loan within a short time thereafter. In a similar manner, when you make a payment, you send a single wire payment directly to the agent for the full amount, and then the agent distributes the payment to each of the lenders.

It is typical for the agent to serve as the swingline lender and as the primary (or only) issuer of letters of credit, if the revolving line of credit includes sublimits for swingline loans and letter of credit issuance.

The agent will take and hold the security interest in your assets in its name, in its role "as agent" for the benefit of all the lenders. The agent will also perfect the security interest in its name, as agent. This avoids a lot of duplicated efforts (and costs), because with this single step, each of the lenders then has the benefit of a perfected security interest through the agent, and none of them has to document things separately.

If you need an amendment or waiver, you'll start by discussing it with the agent. Typically, you'll work out a plan of action with the agent before the other lenders get involved. Once you've decided on what needs to be done (amendment, waiver, consent, etc.) and have negotiated most of the terms of the required document, it will be circulated to the other lenders for their approval. The agent takes care of all the interactions with the other lenders, and will come back to you if there are any major issues that it can't resolve easily on its own. The other lenders are free to contact you directly, too, of course, and occasionally they will. This happens more often when you have a previously established relationship with the other lenders than if they were brought into the deal by the agent and didn't know anyone at the company before.

If the loan goes into default, the agent will typically take the lead in negotiating a workout of the default. Similarly, if the borrower files for bankruptcy, the agent will have the lead role in any court proceedings, acting on behalf of all the lenders. Occasionally there is a disagreement among the lenders as to what to do in a bankruptcy or default situation. Sometimes the agent is the odd one out, holding a different view from the majority of lenders. In these cases, the terms of the loan agreement will help guide the parties in understanding what rights they have to act independently or to require the agent to do what they want.

Other Agents and Sub-Agents

What about all these other "agents"—documentation agents, syndication agents, collateral agents, and others?

In a syndicated deal, there might be several lenders who have titles like "documentation agent," "syndication agent," and the like. You might reasonably expect that the lender who is the documentation agent has responsibility for the loan documents, or that the syndication agent is the one who took charge of syndicating the loan to other lenders. But, to the contrary, these lenders don't have functional roles like the administrative agent, with initial or ongoing responsibilities. Indeed, it's not unusual for the loan agreement to include a statement that these types of agents have absolutely no rights, powers, obligations, or duties under the loan agreement, other than those applicable to all lenders as such.

These titles are usually given by the administrative agent, in consultation with the borrower, to the lenders who made the largest commitments to lend money under the credit facility, in recognition of that level of support. The titles are reported to industry organizations that rank lenders based on certain criteria ("league tables" and the like), and having one of these titles can be meaningful for those purposes. These "agents" may also receive fees, but typically those are one-time fees paid at closing rather than annual fees like the administrative agent receives.

Indemnification; Limitations

The administrative agent has real responsibilities to the other lenders under the loan agreement. As such, it is common for the agreement to include limitations on the agent's liability and indemnification of the agent by the other lenders.

The agent will want the agreement to say that the agent will only do what the agreement expressly says it will do and not other things people might think are implied. Each lender will specifically authorize the agent to act on its behalf to protect its interests and to carry out the requirements of the agreement. The lenders will agree that the agent is not responsible for the effectiveness, validity, or enforceability of the loan documents, or for the financial condition or affairs of the company, or for the company's performance of the agreements. Each lender will be responsible for making its own credit decision and will be expected to obtain and review information about the borrower that it feels is necessary to make that decision.

The agent normally does not take on liability to the lenders for any actions it takes pursuant to the loan agreement, other than for

113

its own gross negligence or willful misconduct (legal terms meant to address bad acts rather than simple mistakes). More to the point, the lenders agree to indemnify the agent for losses or expenses it suffers in its capacity as agent, to the extent the borrower does not reimburse the agent for these. This is important in a bankruptcy proceeding, for example, where the borrower may not be paying the agent's costs and expenses on a current basis. In that case, the other lenders will each have to chip in to reimburse the agent.

The agent is permitted to refuse to act unless a majority of the lenders instruct it to act. Most of the time, unless absolutely necessary to protect the value of the collateral or for some other urgency, the agent will not seek remedies or take other steps against the borrower without clear instructions from the lenders to do so.

Sub-Agents for Collateral

The agent also has the right to appoint sub-agents, and this is fairly common when dealing with certain types of collateral. The agent may appoint a supplemental collateral agent to hold collateral that it can't hold in its own name. For example, in a few foreign countries, only an entity that's incorporated in that country can hold a security interest in assets located in the country, so a local company would need to be appointed as the collateral agent to hold the security interest in that portion of the collateral. Similarly, in a couple of states, you need a local agent within the state to hold a security interest in real estate. The agent may not be able to hold securities (stock certificates, etc.) as collateral, but perhaps one of its affiliates can, so in that case the affiliate will be appointed to serve as a collateral agent to hold the securities. The agent has the ability to appoint any of these as collateral agents for these limited purposes, and those agents will also have rights to indemnification and other benefits under the loan agreement.

Resignation and Removal of the Agent

The agent can usually resign whenever it wants to, with notice to the lenders and the borrower. The lenders will have the right to appoint a successor agent from among their group (someone who is a lender in the deal), but if they fail to do so, the agent can still resign. What happens next depends on what the loan agreement says. If no replacement agent is appointed, usually the lenders will just each act independently (strictly speaking, the lenders are deemed to collectively be the "agent") until they can appoint an actual agent. Unless there are only two or three lenders in the deal, this will be a very undesirable situation, and there will be significant pressure to find a replacement agent quickly.

Sometimes the company has the right to approve the replacement agent, and sometimes not. The original agent is usually selected by the company as a matter of practice, and then that agent syndicates the deal to the other lenders. But, as a legal matter, the agent acts as agent for the lenders, not the company. So, the lenders are the ones with the authority to select the replacement. If the company doesn't like the lenders' choice of replacement agent, it will presumably begin to look for refinancing opportunities so it can get out of the loan. So, there is some pressure (at least, in a good credit situation, though not in a distressed deal) for the new agent to be someone the company finds acceptable.

What if the agent has become difficult to deal with, and the company or the other lenders want to remove it? In the past, it used to be common to have removal provisions in loan agreements, but these days we don't see them very often. Usually you're stuck with the agent you've got. Again, the practical reality is that if the company can refinance the loan with another (friendly) agent, it will just take that route as a way of eliminating the difficult agent. Since both parties understand that this is the case, issues between the agent and company can frequently (though not always) be resolved by mutual agreement.

SECURITY INTERESTS

Security is mostly a superstition.
It does not exist in nature.

~ Helen Keller

PART 4

Chapter 19

Security Agreements

When we talk about security in the context of a loan agreement, we don't mean personal safety or securing our nation's borders from invasion. In this context, we're talking about something far more mundane: liens (security interests) in the company's assets. Nearly every company other than upper-end "investment grade" companies will have a secured loan, backed by a pledge of some or all of the company's assets.

Types of Property

There are different types of property, and there are different ways of obtaining a security interest in each type. The primary categories are real property and personal property.

Real property—land and buildings that the company owns—will be subject to a mortgage in favor of the lender. This works a lot like your home mortgage. The lender will likely purchase title insurance and may require an appraisal, flood certification, and environmental reports such as a Phase I report. Obtaining all of these items takes time and involves several third parties, which may delay closing of the deal. The mortgage is a separate agreement that will be negotiated between the borrower and lender. It will need to be delivered to the lender on the closing date, in proper form for recording at the county recorder's office. In some states, like California, the document is called a "deed of trust" rather than a mortgage, though the content is largely the same.

Some companies have real property that is leased rather than owned. This is frequently the case with office space. Sometimes the lender will determine that the lease itself is a significant asset of the company, especially if it is for below-market rates or if it's a lease of a very unique property for which there is no readily available substitute. If that's the case, the lender may require a leasehold mortgage on the property, which necessitates a memorandum of lease being recorded in the county recorder's office. Because this process is time-consuming and expensive, and requires the landlord to get involved, it isn't usually done unless the lease represents significant value or is strategically significant for the company. Office space leases rarely fall into this category.

Since the process for obtaining and perfecting a security interest in real property varies from state to state, I won't say much more about that here.

Personal property includes pretty much everything else that you own—books and papers, desks and chairs, pens and pencils, computers and software, machinery and equipment, vehicles and boats, intellectual property (trademarks, copyrights, patents, licenses), securities, cash, accounts receivable, inventory, work in process, parts, supplies, and everything else. A security interest in personal property is usually documented with a security agreement.

Extent of Security Interest

Most of the time, the security interest your lender will require is an "all assets" pledge. That means it includes pretty much everything the company owns, at least as to personal property. (Real property may have exceptions for leased properties and in any case will be dealt with separately, as described previously.)

It is possible to grant a security interest in just a portion of your assets, or only certain types of assets. This is how things work for us as individuals, too. Your car loan is secured only by your car, and not by your house or the contents of your bank account. Your home loan is secured only by your home.

In the corporate context, you could also have a real estate loan secured solely by a certain parcel of real estate, or a limited accounts receivable financing secured only by the company's accounts receivable. However, it is most common for a revolving line of credit and term loan to be secured by all assets.

The "All Assets" Grant

To create a security interest in all of the company's personal property, the security agreement will have broad "granting language" providing for the company to grant the lien to the lender. Here's an example:

> Borrower hereby assigns to Secured Party, and hereby grants to Secured Party a security interest in, all of Borrower's right, title and interest in and to all of the personal property of Borrower, in each case whether now or hereafter existing, whether tangible or intangible, whether now owned or hereafter acquired, wherever the same may be located and whether or not subject to the UCC, including, without limitation, the following (the "Collateral"):
>
> (a) all Accounts;
>
> (b) all Chattel Paper;
>
> (c) all Money and all Deposit Accounts, together with all amounts on deposit from time to time in such Deposit Accounts;
>
> (d) all Documents;
>
> (e) all General Intangibles, including all intellectual property and Payment Intangibles;
>
> (f) all Goods, including Inventory, Equipment, and Fixtures;
>
> (g) all Instruments;
>
> (h) all Investment Property;
>
> (i) all Letter-of-Credit Rights and other Supporting Obligations;
>
> (j) all Records;
>
> (k) all Commercial Tort Claims, including those set forth on Schedule 1 hereto; and
>
> (l) all Proceeds and Accessions with respect to any of the foregoing Collateral.

Each category of Collateral set forth above shall have the meaning set forth in the UCC, it being the intention of Borrower that the description of the Collateral set forth above be construed to include the broadest possible range of assets.

If the lender isn't supposed to have a lien on everything, you can remove the items that don't apply and change the opening paragraph to refer to only the specific items listed.

Other Terms

The security agreement will also include several other terms relating to the collateral.

First, it will describe the obligations that are secured. The secured obligations will typically include everything under the loan documents (and, if relevant, swap or hedge agreements), including principal, interest, fees, expenses, and anything else. For subsidiaries, the secured obligations will include their obligations under the guarantees. The description of the obligations will also include any obligations that are declared void in a bankruptcy proceeding, and interest and other amounts that would have accrued after a bankruptcy filing but were prohibited by the court.

The company will make some representations about the collateral, including statements as to where it is located. For certain types of collateral like intellectual property and bank accounts, the agreement will include lists of all the items (or material items) that are part of the collateral. These may be substantially the same as the schedules to the loan agreement that I referred to earlier.

The lender may also require covenants relating to the collateral. There will be a general set of covenants that requires you to take steps necessary to make sure the lender continues to have a perfected security interest in the collateral, and that you will deliver notices, keep records, and do other things necessary to accomplish this purpose. You'll also agree to permit the lender to inspect the collateral.

If you have securities or valuable intellectual property, there may be additional covenants related to those items. For securities, the lender may have the right to vote the stock and to receive dividends if you go into default on the loan. There may also be registration rights provided, in case the lender wants to sell the stock. For intellectual property, there might be a requirement to pursue applications for registration and to take steps to enforce your rights against others. You might also give the lender a license to use the intellectual property, which, for example, would be necessary to keep your manufacturing operations going if you are producing items with trademarked logos on them.

It is typical for the lender to be appointed as the company's "attorney in fact" if there is a default under the loan. This gives the lender the ability to take action in the company's name, and, if necessary, will allow the lender to collect and sell the collateral without the company's cooperation. This provision should never apply absent an event of default, though, as the company needs to be able to operate its business in the normal course without interference.

The security agreement may also include a long list of remedies applicable only to certain types of collateral. Again, securities and intellectual property are examples of types of collateral that sometimes require specific types of remedies. There will also be a description of what the lender can do if it needs to foreclose on and sell the company's assets, and this will include things like having access to the borrower's property, the ability to remove the property from the borrower's locations, the ability to sell the property with minimal notice, and the ability to notify others of the lender's security interest in the property.

The agreement will also have several standard provisions at the back, covering things like reimbursement of the lender's expenses, jury trial waivers, and the like. If the security agreement is for a syndicated loan, there may be some terms establishing the agent's right to act on behalf of the lenders and stating that any replacement agent would automatically be substituted as the secured party under this agreement.

As mentioned previously, sometimes all of these terms will appear right in the loan agreement itself (and it will be called a "Loan and Security Agreement").

If both the company and its subsidiaries are granting security interests in their assets, this can be done in a single agreement that they all sign.

Chapter 20

Perfection and the Effect of Security Interests

Once you have obtained a security interest, you also have to "perfect" it in order for it to be valid and enforceable.

Perfection

To perfect a security interest in most types of personal property, the lender will file a UCC-1 form with the secretary of state in the state where the company is incorporated. For those of you who remember doing this differently in prior years, note that the law changed a few years ago, so that now the UCC-1 is no longer filed in the state(s) where the assets are physically located. The UCC-1 is also filed electronically now and is not signed by the borrower. If the company's subsidiaries have also granted security interests, UCC-1 forms will need to be filed in the subsidiaries' states of incorporation as well.

The UCC-1 form will put other creditors on notice that the lender has a security interest in the assets and, under the law, allows the lender to "perfect" its security interest.

Certain types of assets require additional steps to perfect the security interest. For example, items like vehicles or boats where ownership is evidenced by a certificate of title and is publicly recorded will require the interest to be noted in the public records. The lender may also hold the certificate of title in its vault.

For bank accounts, deposit account control agreements signed by the depositary bank are needed. Securities accounts similarly require securities account control agreements signed by the intermediaries. In order to establish priority of the lender's lien, securities that are evidenced by certificates (the stock certificates for a subsidiary, for example) will usually need to be delivered to the lender, together with a signed transfer power, to be held by the lender during the term of the loan.

If your company produces software programs, a source code escrow may be required. Copyrights require that a copyright mortgage be recorded at the U.S. Copyright Office. Many lenders also choose to record evidence of their security interests in patents and trademarks at the U.S. Patent and Trademark Office.

There are many different types of property that require additional steps for perfection (or to maintain priority of the lien ahead of other secured creditors), so check with an attorney if you are ever in this situation.

If the lender fails to properly perfect its security interest as required by law, the security interest can be invalidated by a court in a bankruptcy proceeding, leaving the lender unsecured. Because this is such a severe penalty, lenders are usually very careful to make sure they have taken all the required steps—at least as to the most important and valuable collateral if not as to everything.

Real Estate

As mentioned, perfection of a security interest in real estate involves recording a mortgage or deed of trust at the county recorder's office in the county where the real property is located. This is true as to any interest in real estate, even if your lien is just on an easement, or on fixtures that are attached to the property (in which case, an additional UCC-1 may need to be filed as to the fixtures), and not the land itself.

Effect of Security Interest

If you have granted a security interest in your assets, beware. This means your lender will have the right to take your assets if you default on the loan. I don't mean to imply that this is a huge problem, though. You probably won't be able to get a loan at all unless you are willing to grant a security interest, so this risk just goes with the territory. Obviously, the best way to reduce this risk is to make sure you are always in compliance with the terms of the loan agreement—and don't go into default!

Still, it's important to be aware that if disaster strikes and there is no good alternative, the lender may be forced to exercise its rights under your security agreement and take all your pledged assets. The lender will need to follow certain procedures in order to foreclose on the company's assets, either as required by law or as required under the loan or security agreement. Foreclosing on things like registered trademarks, leases, subsidiary stock, and factories can be a complicated undertaking. And, at the end of the day, the lender probably isn't really interested in owning all your assets. The lender usually just wants to get its money back.

To maximize value, the lender can arrange for a sale of the assets. Sometimes this is done with the company's cooperation, and the company is sold as a whole "going concern" operating entity. Sometimes the assets are sold off piecemeal, though this can result in lower prices (and less recovery for the lender). There are procedures set forth in the law as to how this can be done, with both personal property and real estate. There is also a procedure for selling assets in a bankruptcy proceeding (called a "363 sale" because section 363 of the bankruptcy code contains the procedures for this type of sale). Enough said about this for now.

Any proceeds that are left over after the sale, after payment to the lender (and other creditors), will be returned to the company.

OTHER LOAN DOCUMENTS

Too often I find that the volume of paper expands to fill the available briefcases.

~ Jerry Brown

Chapter 21

Guarantees

You might be hoping that your work is done when you finish with the loan agreement and security agreement. But, guess what? There's more!

The lender might also require one or more guarantees in support of your loan. A guarantee is a promise by the guarantor that it will pay the loan back or otherwise perform whatever the company promised to perform in the loan agreement. This means that the lender can seek repayment directly from the guarantor without having to do too much else.

If your business is relatively new or has limited resources, the lender might require the shareholders (or just the majority shareholders) to give personal guarantees of the loan. Personal guarantees are usually unsecured, meaning the lender won't take a lien on the individual's personal assets. That said, occasionally the lender will have a lien on a particular asset, such as securities (stock of the borrower that is owned by the guarantor, for example) or a certificate of deposit held by the bank, depending on the creditworthiness of the guarantor and the company. It may be possible to put a cap on the amount of the personal guarantee, but this depends on a number of factors.

If your company has subsidiaries, they will usually be required to guarantee the loan (if they aren't already included as co-borrowers on the loan). This can actually be a good thing for the company. If the subsidiaries guarantee the loan and pledge their assets in support of the loan, the cash flow and assets of those companies can be added to that of the parent company when the lender makes its credit decision. This can make for a more attractive overall picture, with the lender looking at the combined financial resources of all the entities rather than just the parent company. Also, as a practical matter, you will be given more flexibility to move assets back and forth between the subsidiaries and the parent company, and to make intercompany loans and investments, if the lender has a security interest in all the assets and a right to claim its loan amount against any of these companies.

If your company has a holding company above it that owns all of the borrower's stock, as is common for portfolio companies of private equity sponsors, the holding company may be asked to guarantee the loan, or at least pledge the stock of the borrower in support of the loan. A pledge of stock without a guarantee or other rights against the pledgor is sometimes referred to as a "naked pledge" or non-recourse pledge.

Terms

The guarantee will have the following terms.

- » It can be enforced regardless of the bankruptcy of the primary obligor.

- » Obligations owed to the guarantor by the company are not to be collected or otherwise enforced by the guarantor against the company until the primary obligations to the senior creditor are collected.

- » The debt amount can be increased, and the terms applicable to the debt can be modified, without the consent of the guarantor.

- » Since many states have laws that offer protection to guarantors, the guarantor will be required to waive rights it would otherwise have, including, for example, the right to proceed against the company for the amount of the debt, the right to assert defenses based on its or the company's circumstances, and any limitations on its liability. The waivers will also include standard waivers of requirements for demand or presentment, notice of default, and a waiver of defenses based on the statute of limitations. (Sometimes the waiver section is the longest part of the guarantee.)

>> It can be enforced against any one guarantor or all of them, with no right to require other guarantors to pay or to require the creditor to go after the borrower for payment first.

>> Guarantors will be required to pay the creditor's expenses and indemnify the creditor from losses.

Other standard terms will also be included.

There might be separate guarantees for each of the companies, or, as with security agreements, they can all be combined into a single agreement signed by everyone together. Typically, a holding company (parent of the borrower) would sign a separate guarantee from the one the subsidiaries sign. Sometimes this is just for convenience, but it can be for substantive reasons as well, particularly if the holding company guarantee will be limited in scope. The subsidiary guarantee might be separated from the holding company guarantee if it contains additional "savings clauses" meant to protect against the risk that the subsidiary guarantee will be voided as a fraudulent conveyance in a bankruptcy proceeding. This risk is greater with an "upstream" guarantee from a subsidiary company than with a "downstream" guarantee from the holding company, as the courts assume that the shareholders of a company benefit when the company receives a loan, whereas the benefit to a subsidiary isn't as clear. The details here are beyond the scope of this book.

Individual shareholders will each sign separate guarantees, and those guarantees will include other provisions appropriate for individual persons rather than corporate entities.

As mentioned, the guarantees may or may not be secured by liens on the assets of the guarantors.

Chapter 22 ════════════════════════════

Promissory Notes

The role of a promissory note really varies from deal to deal. For smaller debt amounts received from the company's investors, the promissory note may contain all of the terms and may be the sole evidence of the loan. This works fine for relatively simple loan arrangements, and is commonly the practice where the note is supposed to be freely transferable and treated as a bearer instrument.

Bank loans, by contrast, will rarely be documented with a promissory note alone. There is almost always a loan agreement that contains the covenants and other general terms applicable to the loan.

The promissory note is often just a simple one- or two-page document that states the loan amount and that it is payable by the borrower to the lender, "as set forth in the loan agreement"— meaning, go look at the loan agreement for all the actual deal terms (interest rate, payment dates, defaults, remedies, covenants, etc.). Syndicated loans are always documented in this manner, and the issuance of promissory notes will be optional, at the request of the lenders. There are a few lenders who still require promissory notes for their records for each loan they make, but many do not require them anymore. Instead, they will rely on the loan agreement itself as evidence of the debt.

So, it is quite possible to have just a loan agreement and no promissory note at all.

On occasion you'll see a hybrid approach, with some terms stated in the loan agreement and some in the note. This is just an alternative method for drafting loan documents. In this type of loan documentation, the agreement will contain the representations and warranties, covenants, and defaults. The note will contain the loan amount, drawing and repayment terms, interest rate information, and other terms relating to the loan itself (as opposed to things relating to the company). Sometimes the note will contain additional events of default, which can make it a bit confusing, as you'll have to look at both documents carefully to determine all the terms applicable to the loan.

Chapter 23

Intercreditor Agreements

Issues

What happens if you have more than one loan, or more than one kind of debt? This is an interesting question. Some senior lenders will just tell you that you can't have any other debt, and that'll be the end of the story right there. Debt that's in existence when you get a loan from a lender like that will have to be disposed of one way or another (paid off, converted to equity, etc.).

It's often acceptable to the lender if you have some small amount of debt from your shareholders or founders. Founder debt will usually be unsecured and documented on a fairly simple promissory note that doesn't contain a lot of covenants or events of default. It will also usually be long term (not due anytime soon). As long as the note is reasonable in its terms, the lender may be okay with leaving the debt outstanding. Depending on what the note says, there may not be a need for a subordination or intercreditor agreement. Still, most of the time the lender will require that the holders of the existing debt expressly agree to subordinate their loans to the lender's senior debt.

Before we get started, let's make a distinction between lien subordination and debt subordination. Lien subordination is subordination of the security interest in the borrower's assets (and subordination of the right to exercise remedies such as selling the collateral), whereas debt subordination subordinates the right to repayment of the debt itself. It is possible to subordinate just the security interest and not the debt, or to subordinate both.

Subordination Agreements

Like loan agreements, subordination agreements can take many forms. A subordination agreement for a note from a founder or shareholder will likely be short and simple. It will prohibit the investor from placing a lien on any of the company's assets, and will say that the founder cannot receive any payments on any of this debt (other than possibly interest payments, and then only if there is no default under the senior debt). Because the senior lender is providing the "new money" for the company, it will generally insist on being paid out first. The restrictions in the subordination agreement will apply until the senior debt has been paid in full.

The investor will also agree not to seek any remedies against the company based on a breach or default under its note, and will agree not to take any action in a bankruptcy proceeding other than to file a proof of claim as to the amount it is owed. If the investor receives any payments in violation of the subordination agreement, it will hold those in trust for the senior lender, and it agrees to turn the funds over to the senior lender immediately. The agreement will include waivers of many statutory rights the investor would otherwise have and will limit the rights of the investor in many other ways. It will also include a prohibition on amending the promissory note without consent of the senior creditor.

Intercreditor Agreements

The terms "subordination agreement" and "intercreditor agreement" generally mean the same thing and are often used interchangeably. Those of us who regularly work on these are probably more likely to call the document a subordination agreement when it is a simpler form of agreement relating to shareholder/founder debt. Subordination agreements pretty much favor the senior lender. The junior lender simply agrees that its debt will be subordinated in all respects.

Calling the document an "intercreditor agreement" implies that there is going to be some discussion between the creditors and that the terms aren't all one-sided in favor of the senior creditor. The junior creditor will certainly be subordinated in some respects, so the agreement would indeed be a "subordination" agreement in that sense, but there are likely to be exceptions to the subordination and occasions where the terms that restrict the junior creditor are paralleled by terms restricting the senior creditor.

The agreement is also more likely to be called an intercreditor agreement (or even "subordination and intercreditor agreement") when both of the creditors have security interests in the company's assets. In that case, the purpose of the agreement, among other things, is to determine relative priority of the security interests and the creditors' rights in the shared collateral.

Fairly frequently, a subordination or an intercreditor agreement will subordinate the liens on the collateral, but will have very limited subordination of the debt, permitting regularly scheduled payments (but perhaps not voluntary prepayments), unless there is a default on the senior debt.

Some agreements between creditors that both have liens on the company's assets will provide for a full "silent second," meaning that the junior creditor (the holder of the "second" lien) is greatly restricted in what it can do and is expected to sit almost "silently" until the first lien loan is paid. Other agreements include more of a compromise position, restricting the junior creditor but allowing it a few limited rights to assert its interests. A few agreements have an even-handed approach because the creditors have agreed to relatively equal treatment. This is often the case where the creditors are splitting some of the collateral on an equal priority basis—i.e., you'll go first as to the liquid assets (cash, accounts receivable), I'll go first as to everything else, and we'll each have second liens behind each other on those same assets.

The borrower usually doesn't have significant interest in much of the content of the intercreditor agreement. This is not to say that you're not interested in knowing what it says—of course you are. But you won't have much of a say in how most of the terms end up being worked out. As the name implies, the agreement is inter-creditor—i.e., between the creditors. The borrower may be added as a party to acknowledge the content and agree not to behave in a manner contrary to what the agreement says (for example, you'll agree not to send payments to the junior creditor if payments are prohibited under the agreement), but otherwise your role here will be limited. Still, certain terms, such as the length of the standstill period and other limitations on the junior creditor, may be negotiable and are worth inquiring about.

Waiver Issues

Intercreditor agreements are the subject of a lot of negotiation between creditors because the junior creditor is being asked to give up many of the rights it might otherwise have. As compensation for giving up these rights, the junior creditor is usually getting a higher interest rate (or original issue discount, or fees, or a combination of these) from the borrower, given its somewhat riskier position as compared to the senior creditor. The junior creditor probably also recognizes the value and necessity of the senior creditor's loan. If the company needs additional capital, it's good for the company to be able to get those funds at a lower interest rate than the junior creditor would offer. If everything is working as it should, what's good for the company should be good for the creditors.

The most significant waivers the junior creditor is asked to give relate to two things: the junior lender's ability to enforce its loan agreement by seeking remedies against the company, and the junior lender's rights in a bankruptcy proceeding.

Typically there will be a "standstill" period where the junior lender must refrain from taking action in order to give the senior lender the first opportunity to take enforcement actions against the borrower. If the junior loan is in default, the junior lender might have to wait for 180 days or more (the duration of this period is usually highly negotiated) before it can try to collect the debt or take other actions against the borrower. The senior lender, therefore, has the right to control what happens to the borrower's assets first. It's possible for the standstill period to be lengthened almost indefinitely while the senior lender continues its enforcement actions, as long as the senior lender is "diligently pursuing" its enforcement efforts.

The junior lender will also be severely restricted as to what it can do in a bankruptcy proceeding. The junior lender will generally be permitted to file proof of its claim against the borrower, but it usually won't be allowed to object to debtor-in-possession financings that are offered by the senior creditor, plans of reorganization that are supported by the senior creditor, or other actions taken by the senior creditor. The junior lender will also be restricted from arguing that the senior lender should not be given senior treatment in the bankruptcy. And so on, and so on. Again, the senior creditor wants to be able to control the bankruptcy process without interference from the junior creditor, and these waivers help establish that right.

Conclusion ===

Bank loans are complicated. Even for experienced professionals, it can be difficult to navigate your way through the loan process. Certainly, sitting down to read through a 150-page credit agreement written in legalese isn't something most people would look forward to. This book was meant to help you understand the terms of your loan agreement in plain language and, hopefully, to make the loan process a little less painful.

Loans are an important part of our economy. They are extremely helpful in growing and maintaining many types of businesses. Obtaining a loan is always an extremely significant event in the life of a company, and probably will be for your company as well.

Of course, no book can do it all. Though I've tried to cover most of the main issues you'll likely face when getting a loan, this is just a general overview of basic principles. There's really no substitute for the advice of experienced legal counsel who understands your specific business needs and concerns.

I hope you've found this book helpful, and I wish you success in your business endeavors.

Appendix ══════════════════════════════

PAYMENT AND REPORTING REQUIREMENTS

for

CREDIT AGREEMENT

Dated as of [_____]

among [_____]

and [_____]

Terms:

"Administrative Agent" means [_____].

"Borrower" means [_____].

"Closing Date" means [_____].

"Lenders" means [_____]
and other lenders who may be party to the Credit Agreement in the future.

"Loan Parties" means [_____]
the Borrower, and any future Subsidiaries.

*NOTE: Edit the descriptions to match the actual requirements of your credit agreement. Add and delete reporting and payment requirements as necessary. In the left column, fill in the actual calendar date(s) on which each item is due, as well as the method for calculation of each (i.e., "March 25, 2010, 30 days after the Closing Date").

PAYMENTS	
Interest	
WHEN DUE	DESCRIPTION
[Quarterly] on each Interest Payment Date	Interest on the [Revolving Loans and Term Loans] *[See Section_____]* "Interest Payment Date" means [_____.]
Principal	
WHEN DUE	DESCRIPTION
Last day of [each March, June, September, and December, starting with _____]	Principal payment installments with respect to the Term Loans, in the amount of $[_____] each *[See Section _____]*
[_____] (Revolving Maturity Date)	All outstanding amounts under the Revolving Loans *[See Section _____]*
[_____] (Term Loan Maturity Date)	Principal payment of $[_____] (all remaining amounts outstanding) under the Term Loans *[See Section _____]*
Fees	
WHEN DUE	DESCRIPTION
Last day of [each March, June, September, and December]	Revolving Loan Commitment Fee in the amount equal to [__]% of the amount by which the Aggregate Revolving Commitment exceeds the Outstanding Amount of Revolving Loans *[See Section _____]* ["Aggregate Revolving Commitment" means _____.]

Last day of [each March, June, September, and December]	Administrative Agent's fee in the amount of $[_____] *[See Section ___ and Fee Letter]*

Occasional Voluntary Prepayments	
WHEN DUE	**DESCRIPTION**
On or prior to [_____]	If prepaying the loans, a prepayment premium equal to [__]% of the aggregate principal amount of Term Loans so prepaid applies to all [mandatory] prepayments of Term Loans *[See Section ___]*
After [_____] and on or prior to [_____]	If prepaying the loans, a prepayment premium equal to [__]% of the aggregate principal amount of Term Loans so prepaid applies to all [mandatory] prepayments of Term Loans *[See Section ___]*
	Note that voluntary prepayments of Revolving Loans may be made at any time, and no prepayment premium applies.

Occasional Mandatory Prepayment Events	
WHEN DUE	**DESCRIPTION**
[___] days after Fiscal Year end (no later than [_____])	[__]% of the Consolidated Excess Cash Flow for the Fiscal Year last ended *[See Section ___]*
If stated event occurs	If the aggregate unpaid principal amount of all Revolving Loans then outstanding exceeds the Aggregate Revolving Commitments then in effect *[See Section ___]*
If stated event occurs	Asset Sales or Recovery Events - certain proceeds thereof *[See Section ___]*

If stated event occurs	Financing Events - certain proceeds thereof *[See Section ___]*
	Note that any mandatory prepayments due to Asset Sales, Recovery Events, or Financing Events are subject to a prepayment premium as set forth above. *[See Section ___]*

REPORTING REQUIREMENTS

Annual

WHEN DUE	DESCRIPTION
[___] days after Fiscal Year end	A consolidated balance sheet of Borrower and its Subsidiaries as at the end of the Fiscal Year, and the related consolidated and consolidating statements of income or operations, shareholders' equity and cash flows for such Fiscal Year together with a statement of its independent certified public accountants *[See Section ___]*
[___] days after Fiscal Year end	Compliance Certificate with calculations of financial covenants *[See Section ___]*
[___] days after Fiscal Year end	Forecasts prepared by the Borrower, including a forecasted consolidated balance sheet and statements of income or operations and cash flows *[See Section ___]*

Quarterly

WHEN DUE	DESCRIPTION
[___] days after Fiscal Quarter end [1st three Quarters)	A consolidated balance sheet of the Borrower and its Subsidiaries as at the end of such Fiscal Quarter, and the related consolidated statements of income or operations, shareholders' equity and cash flows for such Fiscal Quarter and for the portion of the Fiscal Year then ended *[See Section ___]*

[___] days after Fiscal Quarter end [1st three Quarters)	Compliance Certificate with calculations of financial covenants *[See Section ___]*

Monthly	
WHEN DUE	DESCRIPTION
[___] days after month end	Consolidated statements of income or operations and cash flows for such month <u>and</u> for the portion of the Fiscal Year then ended *[See Section ___]*

Occasional Document Deliveries	
WHEN DUE	DESCRIPTION
When available	Copies of each annual report, proxy or financial statement, or other report or communication sent to the equity owners of the Borrower in their capacity as such *[See Section ___]*
When available	Copies of all reports, registration statements, and prospectuses filed with the SEC or any other regulatory authority *[See Section ___]*
[___] Business Days after receipt	Copies of notices from holders of Subordinated Indebtedness or from trustees, agents, or representatives of such holders *[See Section ___]*
Upon request	Such additional information regarding the business, financial, or corporate affairs of the Borrower and its Subsidiaries, or compliance with the terms of the Loan Documents, as the Administrative Agent or any Lender may reasonably request *[See Section ___]*

If stated event occurs	Notice to Administrative Agent (accompanied by a statement of a Responsible Officer setting forth details of the event and stating what action the Borrower has taken and proposes to take with respect thereto) regarding: • [_____] • [_____] and • [_____] *[See Sections ___]*
[___] days after event	Provide written notice of termination, lapse, or cancellation of insurance *[See Section ___]*
Upon request	Deliver notices of Liens, UCC financing statements, or fixture filings and amendments, keep stock records, obtain waivers from landlords and mortgagees, and pay claims that might, if unpaid, become a lien on any material portion of the Collateral *[See Section ___]*
[___] days after event	If new Subsidiary is formed or acquired, cause such new Subsidiary to execute a counterpart to the Guaranty and Security Agreement and any other instrument that Administrative Agent deems appropriate, and deliver to the Administrative Agent a written notice identifying the Subsidiary and other documents as stated *[See Section ___]*
Upon request	Execute and deliver to the Administrative Agent, from time to time, written statements and schedules as the Administrative Agent may reasonably require regarding the Collateral *[See Section ___]*

Information re Third Parties	
WHEN DUE	DESCRIPTION
If stated event occurs	All lawful claims which, if unpaid, would by law become a Lien upon any material portion of the Borrower's property *[See Section __]*
If stated event occurs	Payment of Indebtedness (other than the Obligations), as and when due and payable, but subject to any subordination provisions contained in any instrument or agreement evidencing such Indebtedness *[See Section ___]*

IMMEDIATE POST-CLOSING REQUIREMENTS	
WHEN DUE	DESCRIPTION
[___] days after the Closing Date	Enter into account control agreements with respect to each of the Deposit Accounts *[See Section ___]*
[___] days after the Closing Date	Execute and deliver documents that the Administrative Agent reasonably deems necessary or advisable to grant perfected first liens in [certain assets] *[See Section ___]*
[___] days after the Closing Date	Enter into and maintain swap contracts for no less than [___]% of the outstanding amount of the Term Loans *[See Section ___]*

For other articles and publications by Susan C. Alker, please visit the Winston & Strawn LLP website:

www.winston.com

Susan frequently writes and speaks on topics related to corporate finance. You can contact her directly at:

Susan C. Alker
Winston & Strawn LLP
333 S. Grand Ave., Suite 3800
Los Angeles, CA 90071

E-mail: salker@winston.com

Susan C. Alker is a partner in the Los Angeles office of Winston & Strawn LLP, one of the largest law firms in the world. As a member of the firm's corporate finance practice, she has extensive experience representing major banks, financial institutions, private equity funds, hedge funds, and corporations in a wide variety of lending transactions. She frequently advises clients in connection with syndicated credit facilities, leveraged acquisition financings, cross-border loans, asset-based loans, debtor-in-possession credit facilities, investment grade loans, and real estate financings. She also represents clients in subordinated debt transactions, including mezzanine loans and second-lien loans, and has expertise in dealing with highly complex intercreditor arrangements for sharing of collateral.

Susan has a JD from the UCLA School of Law and an MBA in international business from the California State University, Los Angeles. Prior to joining Winston & Strawn, she was a member of the corporate finance practice at O'Melveny & Myers LLP and Reed Smith LLP. She frequently writes and speaks on topics of interest to financial institutions. Susan is admitted to practice law in California and New York.